WHEN THINGS GET ROUGH, STAND BY YOUR SPOUSE!

Are you among the whopping 70% of married people who say their marriages are downright bad? Are communication, love, and appreciation missing from your relationship? Now there's hope—without expensive professional help—if you're willing to invest the effort. Using self-questioning techniques, worksheets, behavior "contracts," and specific goal-setting, *How to Save Your Troubled Marriage* can be the most inspiring, most useful tool in achieving the marital bliss you both deserve.

CRISTY LANE has won a total of fifteen gold and platinum awards for her inspirational record albums and a prestigious Academy of Country Music award. Her *One Day at a Time* album became the largest-selling gospel album in the world. She and her husband, Lee Stoller, have built a remarkable musical career together—and an enduring marriage.

LAURA ANN STEVENS, Ph.D., is a licensed Professional Counselor and Director of the Institute for Life and Change, an independent counseling and consulting firm. Her areas of specialization in psychotherapy include individual, marriage and family counseling, as well as stress management, grief therapy, and weight control.

How to SAVE YOUR TROUBLED MARRIAGE

Cristy Lane
and
Dr. Laura Ann Stevens

ST. MARTIN'S PRESS/NEW YORK

HOW TO SAVE YOUR TROUBLED MARRIAGE

Copyright © 1987 by Pygmalion I Limited Partnership

Library of Congress Catalog Card Number: 87-071126

ISBN: 0-312-91360-5   Can. ISBN: 0-312-91361-3

Printed in the United States of America

John Brock edition published 1987
First St. Martin's Press mass market edition/January 1989

10 9 8 7 6 5 4 3 2 1

For our husbands,
Lee and Tom

CONTENTS

INTRODUCTION

Let's face it. Maintaining a happy marriage may be the number one problem for Americans today. Just look at the numbers. Well over 90 percent of adults are still choosing to marry, even in this age of commitment phobia, but about half of them end up divorced. Of those who get divorced, eight out of ten try marriage again, and the divorce rate of these new marriages is even higher than for first marriages!

Even for those who stay married the statistics are dismal. Most studies show that fewer than 15 percent of married people describe their marriages as "very happy." Another third describe their marriages as "happy," which leaves about 50 percent of all marriages (and remember, we are talking only about those who stay married) in moderate or serious trouble. Even these figures are conservative. In a recent survey only 5 percent of married people rated their marriage as great and 25 percent as good. A whopping 70 percent said that their marriages were downright bad!

So what's going on here? It's easy for older people to say that the new generation just doesn't have the sense of commitment that they had, and that they don't know the meaning of "til death us do part." Maybe there's some truth to that. The reality, however, is that there are a lot more pressures on marriages today than a generation ago. To name a few:

—Divorce laws have greatly relaxed. "No fault" divorce is common.

—The high divorce rate alone can cause couples to take the easy way out. The stigma of divorce is gone.

—Couples have higher expectations of marriage. They don't want to settle for less, as their parents sometimes did.

—Our society has placed far too much importance on romantic love. Most marriages today begin with unrealistic expectations. Movies, books, TV, advertising, songs, poems, and commercials constantly make us believe that lovers float away into some happily-ever-after land. Unfortunately, this fantasy has little to do with the reality of the everyday world they will inhabit.

—Much more time is spent outside the home. This multiplies stress.

—The increase in life expectancy means a couple, barring divorce, can expect to celebrate a golden wedding anniversary! That's the longest span for married life in history. Death may have done for our ancestors' marriages what divorce does today.

—Out-of-wedlock pregnancies have induced many to marry who might not otherwise have done so.

—More and more people are marrying outside their ethnic, cultural, and sociological groups, adding extra stress.

—There are more teenage marriages, increasing the risk of divorce.

—Widespread alcohol and drug abuse causes serious marital problems.

—The burgeoning number of women working outside the home, for economic or self-fulfillment reasons, has given rise to the stresses of the dual-career family.

—Divorced parents send the message to their children that divorce is a reasonable answer to a marriage in trouble, which increases the chances that their children will divorce.

—More opportunities for women mean fewer women need to stay in their marriages out of economic necessity.

Yet a happy marriage remains not only what most of us want but what is actually best for us. Research shows us a lot of positive data associated with happy marriages. Happily married people have longer lives, fewer illnesses, higher self-concepts, less stress, fewer suicides (as well as homicides and fatal car accidents), less mental illness, more economic stability, children who do better in school, and on and on. Happily married people do better economically, emotionally, and physically.

As we have seen, however, the factors that affect whether a marriage succeeds or fails are often forces over which the couple has little control. So what's a person to do? Where does one turn for help? Unfortunately, so far there have only been two places: (1) The self-help books on "How to Have a Happy Marriage," which are usually long on nice-sounding platitudes, but short on how to do it. Further these books are rarely aimed at marriages in trouble. (2) The "marriage counselor," sometimes a minister who is usually over-worked and often not qualified, or a professional who usually charges $50.00 or more an hour (and can still be unqualified). As one expert recently stated, "Most therapists are about as poorly prepared for marital therapy as most spouses are for marriage." Marriage counselors, of course, are delighted to see you for ten to fifteen or more sessions, running the cost of marriage counseling to hundreds and sometimes thousands of dollars.

It's easy to see why counselors have helped "mystify" marriage counseling. If counseling is seen as something deep and mystical that only a very highly trained person can do, then the demand for marriage counselors will never decrease. The truth, however, is that there is very little about saving a troubled marriage that the average person cannot understand and apply, without having to spend a small fortune. It is certainly true that there are indeed marriages which, because of severe problems, crises, or even personality disorders, need the involvement of a third party. However, the vast majority of marriages can be helped significantly by applying the easily understood skills and concepts explained in this book.

There are other reasons besides financial for being your own marriage counselor with the help of this book. The majority of people who actually contact a professional are thinking, "The marriage counselor, being the trained person he (she) is, will of course straighten my partner out. The problem is all really within him (her)." A counselor can get hooked into such a collaborative relationship, but a book can't take sides. It can only point out that both of you share the responsibility for the dissatisfaction and also share the responsibility for improving the marriage.

One final advantage: You can't complain to a book! Marriage counselors often get caught in a cross-complaint trap. But marriage counselors aren't in the complaint business; they're in the business of working with couples who are willing to make changes. Since you can't complain to this book, you can only use it to make some real changes in your marriage.

This book seeks to provide you with the skills, principles, habits, and insights that you can use to help your own troubled marriage. They are based on solid research, an accepted body of knowledge within the field of marriage counseling, and material from hundreds of couples counseled over the years. The following chapters will address such issues as:

—Exactly what is and what isn't "marriage counseling"? What can we expect and what do we have to do?

—How do we get beyond the fear, anger, and pride in order to make real changes?

—What if my spouse won't change? Can I do it alone?

—How do we identify exactly what our goals for this marriage are?

—How do we immediately start focusing on giving and receiving positive, caring behaviors instead of negative ones?

—How can I really share my feelings safely with my spouse and get him or her to do the same?

—How can we express negative feelings without aggressiveness and without making our partner defensive?

—Exactly how do we negotiate the conflict, the bad problems, and incompatibilities in this marriage?

—How do we stop our "dirty fighting"?

—How do we keep reenacting our parents' marriages? And how can we change that if it's not appropriate?

—How can we uncover the real issues behind the surface fights?

—How can we learn to live with what we can't change?

—How can I "fall in love" again if I don't love my spouse?

—How can we nurture our relationship so we don't get into serious trouble again?

—How can we solve our sexual problems and make our sex life exciting again?

—Where do we go if more help is needed?

We don't claim that this book has all the answers. Human beings and marriages are much too complex to fit nicely into one book. However, this book is almost certain to provide you with the encouragement, skills, and insights to help change your marriage into the one you truly want, if you are willing to put forth the effort. Here's wishing you many years of marital bliss!

GUIDELINES FOR THE USE OF THIS BOOK

The following guidelines may make using this book easier and more meaningful. These guidelines, however, are not set in concrete. You may find that some other method or time frame works better for you, and that's all right. Different couples have different constraints, with time and other factors, and this must be taken into consideration.

You might want to read the whole book before you start doing any of the suggested activities. This is perfectly all right and can give you a sense of the feeling of the book as a whole. However, when you actually start using the book to improve your marriage, it is important that you proceed much more slowly. Various skills and concepts must be initiated, discussed, and *practiced* before you can go on to more advanced concepts. If you don't take the time to practice the skills and activities you will not be making them a habit. That means they will not become a part of you or a part of your marriage and any changes will be superficial and temporary. We give you a suggested time frame, and though that may need to be adjusted by individual couples, there will be some real drawbacks from varying too widely.

Quite obviously two persons can't read this book

at the same time. We would like to suggest, therefore, that one partner read one chapter, then give it to the other partner to read within twenty-four hours. After both of you have read the chapter you come together to discuss the concepts and practice the skills. After you have practiced for about a week, start on a new chapter and repeat the process. One partner reads the next chapter; the other reads it within twenty-four hours, then both meet to discuss and practice.

SUGGESTED TIME FRAME

The following is a suggested time frame for using this book. Feel free to adapt this to your particular situation. However, if you go much faster than this, you're greatly increasing your chances of forgetting or ignoring the material. All research on learning shows that information learned quickly and not practiced or reinforced is quickly forgotten. Information learned more slowly and practiced, reviewed, or reinforced is usually more permanent. However, there is also a danger in progressing much more slowly than the suggested time frame. Again, you are likely to forget, unless you constantly review the information. If, as is more often the case, you do nothing during large gaps in the program, you will critically damage your motivation and progress. If you must go longer than the recommended time between sections of this program, you should go back and review what you have already learned and done.

Week Number   1—Introduction, Chapter 1, Chapter 2
               Discuss all concepts at length with each other. Notice and discuss daily how they apply to you. Fill out Goals Worksheets and make couple goals.

Week Number   2—Chapter 3—"Valuing" and "Catch Your Partner Pleasing You"
               Do recommended activities daily.

Week Number   3—Chapter 4—"Sharing Feelings"
               Do recommended activity daily.

Week Number   4—Chapter 4—"Active Listening"
               Do recommended activity daily.

Week Number   5—Chapter 4—" 'I' Messages"
               Do recommended activity daily.

Week Number   6—Chapter 5—"The Echo Game"
               Practice the Echo Game daily.

Week Number   7—Chapter 5—"Other Helpful Messages"
               Do recommended activity daily.

Week Number   8—Chapter 6—"Hurtful Messages"

Do recommended activities daily.

Week Number 9—Chapter 6—"The Fair Fighting Process" and "Fair Fighting Rules"
Conflict Negotiation: Stage 1 and 2
Read several times and discuss until understanding of process is assured.
Chapter 7—"When the Spouse Keeps Attacking or Defending," "Marital Scripts"
Do recommended activity.

Week Number 10—Chapter 7—"Solving Your Own Problems"
Do recommended activities daily.
Uncovering the Real Issues: Read and discuss.

Week Number 11—Chapter 8—"The Marital Contract"
Do recommended activity.
"What to Negotiate, What to Ignore"
Read and discuss.

Week Number 12—Chapter 9—"Nurturing the Love Relationship," "What is Love?" "Reciprocity Reviewed," "List of Loving Things to Do," "Down Memory Lane"
Discuss all concepts at length.

Do recommended activities daily.

Week Number 13—Chapter 9—"The Oxygen of Intimacy" "Time," "Talk," "Touch"

Discuss all concepts at length.
Do recommended activities daily.

Week Number 14—Chapter 10—The Sexual Relationship

Discuss all concepts at length.
Do recommended activity if appropriate.

Week Number 15—Chapters 11 and 12

Discuss all concepts at length.

WHEN ONE PARTNER WON'T COOPERATE

Perhaps you are dissatisfied with your marriage, but your spouse will not cooperate with making it better. Perhaps he/she is actually "happy" in the relationship and thinks the marriage doesn't need help. Perhaps he/she is dissatisfied but is saying, "There's nothing wrong with *me!* I don't need marriage counseling. I'm not going to read that book." Perhaps he/she just doesn't seem to care. You may be asking yourself "Can I do it alone?" "Is there any point in my reading and using this book if my spouse won't?" "Will this book help if my partner says he/she won't change?"

The answer is a resounding "Yes!" If you read

and use the principles outlined in this book, it will be almost impossible for your marriage not to improve. As you will see in the next two chapters, all marriages are "systems," with the parts so interrelated that a change in one causes a change in both. It is impossible for you to change significantly without your partner also changing. If you increase your awareness, communications skills, affection, etc., you will almost always see changes in your partner. And when your partner sees positive changes in you brought about by this book, he/she may be motivated to read it him/herself.

If you have read and put into practice all the concepts and skills presented in this book for a period of several months and still do not see any significant change in your spouse, refer to the final chapter, "When More Help is Needed." You may be in a situation that calls for professional counseling.

CHAPTER 1

What is Marriage Counseling?

Welcome to *How to Save Your Troubled Marriage*. Before you journey down the path of being your own marriage counselor, it's important to have a good understanding of what marriage counseling is and is not. It doesn't matter if you go to a marriage counselor or become your own marriage counselor through the use of this book. There are certain things that characterize marriage counseling and some that do not.

WHAT MARRIAGE COUNSELING IS

There are several things that marriage counseling focuses on. The most important of these is the time frame of your focus.

A Focus on the Present and Future

As of now your focus is on the present and future —*not* the past. As a matter of fact, we are going to have to put up a chain link fence (with a barbed-wire top) between the past and the present, one that you can't cross under, over, or through! Yes, we know that the past is where all these problems originated, (and where your ungrateful spouse did all those obnoxious things to you), but that's over and done with. Even God can't change the past. The only thing you can do is start this very day and ask "What can we do *now* to make it better?" Concern with the past will lead only to blaming and defensiveness. It will *not* solve your problems. Until you get this idea clearly in your head, you will stay on a merry-go-round of attack, defend, counterattack or retreat. So memorize these sentences: "That's over with now. What can we do today to make things better?" Every time your spouse drags up the past say these sentences. Also say them to yourself if you are tempted to drag up the past.

You can't head toward the west without turning your back on the east. You can't head toward the future without turning your back on the past!

Another important concept is that we will focus on skills, real techniques that you can learn to make your marriage better. This is the best approach to use with a book, but it's also attractive because it *works.*

A marriage counselor can use several different approaches, and you may have been exposed to these in the past, or will be in the future. "Psychoanalytic" counselors are primarily interested in the past. They are concerned with each spouse's childhood, "unconscious" problems, relationship to parents, and those parents' relationships to each other. Although we will ask you to look at your parents' relationships, it's obvious the psychoanalytic approach requires a trained counselor.

Another approach is the "systems" approach, which can involve an entire family. It assumes a family is a complex system in which the whole is not just the sum of its parts, but an integrated whole. The parts of the system are so interrelated that a change in one causes changes in all. Relationships are circular and continuous, with no beginning or end. Thus, each person's behavior affects everyone else, often in a chain reaction. This approach also obviously requires a counselor.

A third approach, the "social learning" approach, deals with skills that we learn in society. These skills include those used in communication, problem solving, conflict negotiation, contracting or "exchanging behaviors," and increasing or renewing loving feelings and intimacy. Research shows that this approach is the most effective in working with couples. Thus, the social learning approach is the one used in this book.

This book can help you go a long way in learning these skills—without the help of a counselor. But the skills this book teaches you are only the beginning of your learning. Compare it to driving. Remember when you got your driver's license? You probably weren't a very good driver, although you knew the basic skills. You had to practice the skills under all kinds of conditions for thousands of miles before you were a competent driver. Similarly, your marriage will get better and better for years as you practice the skills in this book.

A Focus on Behavior

For this reason it is important to understand the third focus of marriage counseling—a focus on behavior. We mean observable, specific behavior. We're going to concentrate on what you and your spouse do, not what you are or what you think. When you get right down to it, behavior is really what you want to change, isn't it?

There are a number of reasons why it is important to focus only on behavior:

—It is a difficult, if not impossible, task to change how your spouse thinks, or his or her basic personality.

—Specific behaviors can be easily defined, observed, and measured. This way you can readily tell if your efforts are being successful or not!

—The hidden meaning and assumptions when we speak in terms of global personality factors can lead to confusion and misunderstanding.

—Attacks on someone's character can become self-fulfilling prophecies. If you keep calling me lazy, I will fulfill that prophecy and act lazy.

—Descriptions of personality defects will be experienced as an attack, which will lead to defensiveness or counterattack.

—Specific behavior addresses things that can be changed. If you ask me to call you if I'm going to be late I know what you want. If you call me "inconsiderate," I might not know.

—Focusing on behavior works!

WHAT MARRIAGE COUNSELING IS NOT

Just as it is important to know what marriage counseling is, it's important to know what it is *not*. To begin with, it is not finding fault or assigning blame. The concepts of fault or blame have absolutely no place in marriage counseling. Some of the reasons for this are:

—Determining who caused a situation is irrelevant nine times out of ten. There is no courtroom or judge whose decision as to who's at fault will make a whit of difference.

—Blame and faultfinding keep the emphasis on why things are like they are instead of how they can change. Perhaps your spouse did something "wrong." Well, humans frequently do wrong things. What can you do to see that it doesn't occur again?

—Blame and faultfinding keep the emphasis on the past instead of the future.

—Where does the blame stop? If I am shaped by my environment and heredity, shouldn't you blame my parents for producing me? And their parents for producing them? Or maybe their teachers, friends, bosses, etc.

—Blame and fault assume that people and their behaviors can be easily assigned to rigid "good" or "bad" categories. Yet philosophers have argued that "goodness" or "badness" are often more situational than absolute. Even when something is universally thought of as "bad" (lying, stealing), virtually all of us will rationalize our behavior by finding "good" reasons to do the "bad" thing.

—Blame and fault lead to self-rating and other-rating, which are basically irrational and lead to anger and depression. I may have acted "badly," but that doesn't mean I'm "bad."

—Blaming almost always leads to anger or defensiveness, which gets in the way of problem solving.

—If I blame you for your imperfections, then I must blame myself for mine, and the whole human race for theirs. If I think this is okay, I'm essentially saying nobody can be human. How grandiose and perfectionist can I get?

Blame is the ultimate copout. If I insist that everything is your fault, then I never have to take responsibility for what I do.

Please notice that there is a difference between responsibility and blame. I have to be responsible for my behavior. If I caused an unfortunate situation to occur, I need to realize that I am responsible for the consequences. Seeing the relationship between my behavior and its consequences is critical. But that doesn't mean it helps for me to be condemned and blamed for my behavior.

Perhaps an analogy is in order. If you see a forest fire, which question is more important: "Who started the fire?" or "How can we put it out?" Let's start putting out the forest fires!

Finally, marriage counseling is not a "medical model" where the responsibility for change is on the healer. When we are sick we go to a doctor who gives us medicine to make us well. It's up to the doctor to fix us. That's definitely not the case here. The responsibility for improving your marriage is yours. This book is not a magical medical elixir— finish reading and you'll have a better marriage. Don't be a victim of "magic thinking." Some examples of magic thinking are: (1) I can stop smoking or drinking anytime; (2) This fourth donut won't show; (3) I won't get cancer; (4) I won't go through the windshield; (5) The boss will get better; (6) I can have a better marriage just by reading this book. You *won't* have a better marriage just by reading this book. If you just read this book and do nothing else, your marriage won't change. It takes time, work, effort, practice, and energy to change a marriage. A successful marriage is like a successful anything else: It takes work. Marriages work for those who work at them! A truly happy marriage is never an accident; it always involves a great deal of effort.

If the medical model doesn't apply to marriage counseling, what does? Consider the "piano lesson model." If you take a piano lesson once a week and never practice, you won't learn to play the piano. Instead you practice all week what the teacher taught you, then come back for further instruction. Also, the teacher doesn't start out teaching you to play a concerto. You start learning to play some simple scales. So it is with this book. You will learn some simple skills and concepts that you need to practice diligently. As you progress the skills will become more complex, and you will become more proficient! Here's hoping you learn to play the concerto!

Remember, a counselor is never the determining force in the outcome of counseling. The real force for change is within the couple. A counselor can be a catalyst for change—sometimes necessary, never sufficient—but so can this book. A catalyst can't work alone: What happens depends on you!

CHAPTER 2

Guiding Principles

There are a number of principles that guide marriage counseling that you need to understand as you work through this book.

PRINCIPLE 1

Your Success Is Determined
By Your Commitment

Your success at improving your marriage depends almost entirely on one thing—your commitment! By that we mean how much you want to save your marriage. Understand what we are saying. Improvement in your marriage does not depend on how many problems you've got, how long you've been married, how many years you've been fighting (or so alienated you don't even fight), or even if you think you don't love your spouse anymore. It depends on how badly you want to stay married, for *whatever reasons!* If you are really committed and want to improve your marriage and are willing to work at it, you will be successful. If not, you won't. It's that simple.

Because this is marriage counseling, the assumption is that a willing commitment to remain married is your goal! But commitment is a matter of priorities. No matter how many things you have to do, you manage to do the ones you've given the highest priority. If you want a good marriage badly enough, you will give it high priority. If you give it high priority, you'll succeed.

Picture a scale from 1 to 10. A 10 means that you really want this marriage to work and will do whatever it takes to make it work. A 1 means that you really don't give a rip. Now put yourself on this scale. If you are 7 or above, continue with this book. If you are below 7, you have some decisions to make because this book probably won't help you. All marriage counselors are familiar with people who come to counseling because they want to show their family and friends, "Look how hard I tried." But all the time their eyes are on the door. They want out. Obviously marriage counseling won't work with such people. So using this book won't work if it's used just to get your spouse off your back.

Let us tell you one thing while you're making up your mind what you want, however. Be brutally honest about whether you're suffering from the "greener grass syndrome." If we had a nickel for every person who has told us "If I had known then what I know now, I would have tried harder," we'd be rich. The color of the grass on the other side of the fence is not even important; the grass isn't even edible. The bottom line: The best marriage for you is probably *the one you are in right now!*

PRINCIPLE 2

Expect Resistance due to Hurt, Anger, Pride

You will meet resistance because of three factors: hurt, anger, and pride. These are inevitable! You may have been badly hurt by something your partner did; the pain can be very real, even physical. Sometimes it seems impossible to see behind it. Or you may be so angry that all you can think about is revenge. You feel entitled to your pound of flesh. "It's not fair that he/she shouldn't have to pay!" Or maybe it's pure pride. "How could he/she do such a thing to me? I can never forgive that." All these feelings are normal and almost unavoidable. But they will never help you improve your marriage. They will always get in your way. You have the power to set aside these feelings if you give yourself permission to do so. Let's symbolically do that right now.

Take a big sheet of paper and write down all the hurts that have come your way, all the anger you are feeling, all the statements that capture your hurt pride. Now roll this paper up in a ball, put it in the fireplace, and light a match to it! As it disappears in the flames, say good-bye to these feelings. Any time these feelings start to come back, picture the fire again in your mind. Remind yourself you have told these feelings good-bye and have burned them.

You may have other uncomfortable feelings as you work on your marriage. Don't let them throw you. It's never comfortable to change old habits, and because change is your major goal, the process you're about to go through will sometimes be uncomfortable. Again, discomfort is unavoidable! The absence of discomfort is a sure signal that the change is superficial.

PRINCIPLE 3

Changes in Behavior Precede Changes in Feeling

This must be one of the best-kept secrets in psychology because so few people seem to know it. Most of us think we do something because we like it. We eat ice cream because we like it. We play tennis because we like to. We act loving because we feel loving. While all this is true, it is equally true the other way around. We like ice cream because we have eaten it. We like to play tennis because we have played it. Most important, we feel loving because we have acted loving. It is important to remember this —especially if you feel as if you don't love your spouse as much as you once did. If you begin to act loving, those loving feelings will return.

Acting loving will be especially difficult for two reasons. The most important is that you just don't feel like it. You probably feel decidedly unlike it! You might even think that you would rather hug a cobra than your spouse! (If so, think of it like taking medicine; you've got to do it to get better.) You might also feel "phony," as if you are acting or pretending to feel something you don't. That's OK! It's like wearing new clothes. A new outfit can certainly make you feel and act differently, but you're not being phony—you're still you. Trying on a new role can also make you feel differently. The main thing to remember is that your feelings will come after your behavior changes. Social psychologists have long called this the "as if" strategy. If we behave as if something is true or as if we feel a certain way, then that becomes reality. Remember, change the way you act first, even if you don't feel like it. Soon you will feel like it!

PRINCIPLE 4

Each Spouse Must Change First

Both of you must be willing to be the first to change. It is vitally important that your behavior is not dependent upon your spouse's behavior.

We know your pride can get in the way here. It's easy to think, "Why should I be nice to him while he's still being so ugly to me?" Or, "Why should I even try to reason with her since she's still screaming at me?" Well, let us tell you why. You have *absolutely nothing to lose.* Changing first may be unfair, but it's in your own self-interest. In the first place, it can get you the changes you want in your marriage. Remember, we said marriage is a system. That means the parts of the system are so interrelated that a change in one causes changes in all. So you cannot change without your partner changing. For example, if one of you says something different during a recurring argument, the other can't respond in the same old way.

The system called marriage will virtually always be interactional with both partners counterbalancing. The more he withdraws, the more she pursues. The more she pursues, the more he withdraws. The more she criticizes, the more he defends. The more he defends, the more she criticizes. The more he yells at the kids, the more she spoils them. The more she spoils them, the more he yells at them. So it doesn't matter who started what, you must take responsibility for contributing to it. If you diagram those examples you get: the more he does X, the more she does Y, the more he does X. Either can obviously break the circle by substituting "less" for "more." Changing yourself will have to change your spouse.

Second, even if change doesn't occur, you've still come out ahead. You have learned the skills and concepts that make for a healthy relationship and have grown in the process. Most important, you are now in control of your behavior. This is probably the most important mental health concept there is. Mentally healthy persons are the masters of their fate, not the victims. They don't let it happen, they make it happen. They call the shots in their lives.

They are self-directed, not other-directed. If you let another person's behavior determine yours, you are other-directed. If you respond in a certain way because your spouse acted in a certain way, you are being directed by your spouse. Your behavior is dependent on his or her behavior. That does not leave you in control of your life.

Remember, it's to your advantage to start interacting in healthy ways, regardless of what your spouse does. Your behavior must be "unlatched" or noncontingent, that is, not dependent on your spouse's behavior. If you are saying "I won't change until my spouse changes," it's obvious neither of you will change. Each of you must be willing to change first!

PRINCIPLE 5

Change is Neither Fast nor Direct

The assumption that things will be fine within a few days (or even a week or two) is usually a marriage counselor's number one frustration. Things will not be "fine" within a few days. That is a totally unrealistic expectation. Your marriage did not get into trouble overnight. It will not get out of trouble overnight. Marriages usually get into trouble after months and years of negative patterns of relating to one another. So change will neither be fast nor easy. Your marriage could even get worse before it gets better. You might be expressing some dissatisfactions, hurt feelings, and misunderstandings that you've never shared before. Furthermore, change never occurs in a straight line. There will be some advancing, then retreating, then advancing again. Compare it to a stock market graph. The stock market never goes straight up. There are always a lot of dips. You will also experience these dips—maybe a big blowup, or retreating behind a wall of hurt and silence, or even behavior that is unconsciously testing your spouse. Remember negative habits are hard to unlearn. Backsliding is to be expected. Unfortunately the discouragement after setbacks is usually worse than before you started. You feel helpless and hopeless. You think, "It's no use. We're back to square one again." But if you become discouraged and give up during one of your dips, you will lose sight of your overall progress. That's not fair either to you or the concepts presented in this book!

Identifying Major-Change Goals

Let's take a moment and try to identify some major-change goals you have for your relationship. Change is hard to accomplish unless you have a clear idea of what change you would like. Look at the two Goals Worksheet pages in the appendix. Each of you should fill out your sheet independently. Put a check in the column beside the specific issue if you believe your marriage needs change in that area. If everything is fine in that category, write "OK."

Now write down what specific changes you would like to see occur in your relationship in that area. Remember to stick with behaviors. Get away from the notion that you are going to change the personality of your spouse. Unless somebody knows something about genetic restructuring that we don't, that's going to be impossible! As much as possible, try to think of changes you would like to see in your relationship, not just your spouse.

Finally, prioritize the changes you would like in the column "Rank order of importance." Number 1 will be the change you want most, number 2 the next, and so on.

Now come together with your spouse, share your pages, and try to come up with a list of goals that both of you can agree on. Write your goals on a separate piece of paper. This will not be difficult if you phrase the goals in terms of the relationship. For instance, "to have a more satisfying sex life" would probably be agreeable to both partners, while "to make love more often" would probably cause resistance in one. "To agree on and abide by a budget" would be better than "for my wife to stop spending so much money." If you cannot agree on all of your goals don't worry about it now. You may write separate goals on the paper.

Fold up the piece of paper you have written your goals on, put it in a box, and label the box "The Back Burner." Now put that box out of sight for the time being. We are going to forget about the issues until you learn the skills necessary for solving your problems. The process must come before the content! In our experience marriages that have been the most successful in resolving conflict have invariably been less concerned in the beginning with content (what the conflict is about) than with process (going through the process of working out a solution to the problem).

If you are tempted to argue about or try to solve your problems, remember you have symbolically put them on the back burner while you learn the skills necessary for solving them. Trust us. We will return to them in good time.

CHAPTER 3

Valuing and Appreciation

We're now going to switch our focus from the negative things about your marriage to the positive. One of the first things that breaks down when a marriage starts getting into trouble is openly valuing and appreciating each other. Yet this is one of the most important cornerstones of a healthy marriage. As partners in a marriage affirm, value, and express appreciation for each other, there is an increase in self-esteem for each person. The marriage becomes stronger and the couple experience the intimacy and togetherness they desire. As partners are put down, criticized, and discouraged, they begin to feel inadequate and inept, with a decrease in self-esteem. This leads to the inability or disinclination to value the other spouse. The marriage becomes weaker, and the partners more and more alienated.

Whether you call it compliments, strokes, "warm fuzzies," encouragement, appreciation, or what, *openly valuing your spouse is one of the most important things you can do to keep your marriage happy!*

Take a moment now and write down five things that you like, value, or appreciate about your spouse. They can be large, global concepts like "high integrity," or small things like "I like the way you wrinkle your nose when you smile." You may also list something you like or enjoy in the relationship. After each of you has done this, share what you have written with your spouse. As you do this, discuss when the last time was that you heard these things, whether you have told your spouse these things lately, whether there were any surprises, and most important, how it felt hearing these things.

Assignment

Your assignment now is to tell your spouse at least once a day something you value or affirm in him/her. No matter how angry, hurt, or tired you are, you must express appreciation or affirmation to your spouse every day. This is the marital growth vitamin —your marriage can't grow without it. Just as a plant looks to the sun for its energy, we look to our spouses for our energy to grow. You wouldn't try to make a plant grow by pulling on it. You can't get people to grow by pulling on them. You will define how your spouse sees him/herself just as certainly as if you held up a full-length mirror. You function as your spouse's mirror, and that reflection will affect every aspect of your marriage. Husband, your wife needs to hear from you what you admire about her, what you appreciate about her, what you value in her. Wife, your husband needs to hear the same from you! Incidentally, the simple phrase "I love you" is still the most effective way of telling your partner how special he/she is.

This simple technique alone will have amazing results. You will never, never change your spouse by harping on his/her negative characteristics. A heavy dose of positives works wonders. Dwell on the good! Praise your spouse daily!

CATCH YOUR PARTNER PLEASING YOU

Closely related to verbal appreciation is noticing positive and negative behaviors. Distressed couples are usually in a cycle of negative communication about what each didn't do. Partners are so wrapped up in their dissatisfactions that the positive behaviors are ignored. Yet marital happiness is the result of each spouse's having needs met through positive behaviors and reciprocity—you get what you give and you give what you get. When Mary does and says things that please Jim, he experiences the relationship as rewarding and will be more likely to do and say things that please Mary. And so it goes.

Take a moment now and make a list of ten things you do that please your partner and ten things he/she does that please you. We will call these things "pleasers." A pleaser is any word, phrase, action, behavior, or favor of one that pleases the other.

After your lists are completed, the wife should read aloud her list of ten things she does that please her husband. Then the husband reads aloud his list of ten things she does that please him. Then discuss the following:

1. Are the lists similar, or are you way off base as to what pleases your partner? Often couples in trouble demonstrate an astonishing lack of awareness of the things that please each other. Wife, did your husband list things you had no idea he liked?

2. Do you even know the *category* of things that please your partner? Often one person thinks his/her partner likes the "loving" behaviors, like a good-bye kiss, when the partner would prefer the garbage to be taken out!

3. Are your lists worded in vague or general terms such as "She's a good mother" or specific behavior language as "She helps the children with their homework?" It's important to describe pleasers in concrete and observable terms.

Now switch off, read the other two lists, and discuss the same questions.

Assignment

Your homework assignment is to reinforce your partner once a day for doing or saying something that pleases you. Do this immediately after the pleasing behavior occurs. Examples are: "I love it when you hold hands with me." "It really makes me happy when you feed the baby." "It pleases me when you call me during the day to see how I am." "I sure do appreciate your picking up the laundry for me."

Every day record one pleaser received that day from the other and share that written record with your partner at the end of the day. You are "catching your partner pleasing" and reinforcing him/her for it twice: once when it occurs (this is critical!) and once at the end of the day. We have included a form for "Catch Your Partner Pleasing You" that you can copy. You will need many copies of it.

The purpose of this exercise is to increase pleasing behavior through positive reinforcement. The only way we know to increase human behavior is to reinforce it when it occurs! When both spouses frequently give pleasers to each other, a positive spiral is begun in which the pleasers of one spouse reinforce the pleasers of another. As you can see, though it is important to do the things that please your partner, it is *more* important to let your partner know when he/she has done something to please you. The importance of this exercise cannot be overemphasized. An increase in marital satisfaction depends much more on an increase in positive behaviors than a decrease in negative behaviors.

Concentrate for at least a week on the "Catch Your Partner Pleasing You" exercise before going on with this book. Remember, all those issues you want to resolve are still on the back burner. There will be plenty of time to get them out and solve them later. For right now, just enjoy each other, try to please each other physically and emotionally, and build up good feelings to get ready for the hard work ahead.

Caution: putting a "zinger" on the end of a pleaser will backfire. "That was a great meal, for a change" will do more harm than good.

Keep in mind that pleasers fall into a number of categories and that your spouse determines what pleases him/her. Follow your partner's lead! For some people, the things that please fall in the category of helping with chores or other actions not directly related to the relationship. For others it's the affectionate, loving things that please. Often it's a combination of the two. If you need help with thinking of loving things to do, check the list on page 134 under "Nurturing the Love Relationship."

Because you can only reinforce behaviors that occur, what do you do when your partner doesn't do anything that pleases you? Be assured that it's OK to ask for pleasers. Your partner doesn't have a crystal ball. "I'd really love a hug right now" is a legitimate, desirable request. Occasionally people have quite a bit of difficulty in verbalizing what pleases them. If this is true for you, it may be that your spouse doesn't know what pleases you. A good crutch in this case is the use of poker chips! Give a blue poker chip to your partner when he/she does something that pleases you, a white chip when you recognize it's a good try that doesn't quite make it, and a red chip for something that is definitely not appreciated!

It is common to want to stop this exercise after a few days or weeks. You may think that you understand how it works, that it is boring, or that it seems too "artificial." Never mind. Continue with this exercise for as long as you are using this book. This is one instance when you want to overlearn. You are making a habit of one of the most important behaviors that ensure a happy marriage.

CHAPTER 4

Communication Skills

*Congress is so strange. A man
gets up to speak and says
nothing, nobody listens, and
then everybody disagrees.*

—Will Rogers

We now come to the heart of the book: how to communicate in positive, life-giving ways in a marriage. The term itself, "communication," is probably the most overused, yet least understood, word we use in discussing marriage. Everybody communicates about communication. It has been said that communication is to a marriage what breathing is to life. Certainly it is the lifeblood of a marriage—the most powerful factor determining its success. When communication breaks down, marriages break up!

There is no area of marriage that communication does not affect. When couples communicate effectively they are able to pick up on potential problems before they are serious, solve problems once they present themselves, and increase the intimacy that nourishes their love. To have a relationship, you must relate! Logical, isn't it? Yet so many couples, while crying out for "good communication," aren't able to communicate. Husbands and wives talk at each other, past each other, through each other, but rarely *with* each other. They share the same house and even bed but rarely the same wavelength. Incredibly enough, a recent study showed that the average couple spends only seven minutes weekly talking to each other!

Admittedly, good communication in a marriage does not come easily. There are dozens of things that get in the way, such as faulty perception, negative patterns role modeled from family background, strong emotions, and confusing nonverbal signals. Yet we can learn to communicate. The key word here is "learn." It is not automatic. It is easy to think that because we learned to talk and hear automatically, that we automatically learn to communicate. That makes as much sense as saying if I can sit on a piano bench I can automatically play a concerto. Good communication is as much a set of learned skills as is playing the piano, skiing, or riding a bicycle! Just as you have to practice these things in order to learn them, you will need to practice the skills in this book until they become habit. The good news, however, is that repeated practice will make these skills a matter of instinct and habit. They will become a "part of you!"

SHARING FEELINGS

> *The greatest compliment that was*
> *ever paid me was when one*
> *asked me what I thought, and*
> *attended to my answer.*
>
> —Henry David Thoreau

We believe that the most important communication skill in a relationship is the ability to share feelings—positive feelings, negative feelings, scary feelings, hurt feelings, angry feelings, whatever feelings that are there! There is, incidentally, no way to avoid communicating feelings. If a feeling isn't talked out, it will be acted out—through depression, illness, sexual problems, withdrawing, etc. You may as well share them positively and verbally rather than negatively.

If you don't share feelings verbally, there is little your spouse can do to know you or make intelligent reactions. Your partner will have to go on what he/she makes up—and this is almost always in error. The open mutual expression of feelings is essential in a truly intimate marriage. If both of you are willing to reveal your true selves, your relationship will deepen. If not, you have settled for a superficial relationship.

There are powerful factors that work to prevent us from sharing feelings, however. Essentially, expressing feelings takes courage: It is a risky business.

We risk rejection when we reveal ourselves. It is much easier to play a game, hoping to be loved for what we pretend to be. Probably deep within most of us are doubts about ourselves and about whether we are worthy of love.

Men especially are powerfully conditioned not to express their feelings. Our culture has decreed that it is "feminine" and "sissy" for boys to have feelings. Parents of both sexes seem to encourage this. It is OK to have a tomboy daughter, but not a sissy son! Wives need to understand and be sensitive to the difficulty their husbands may have in sharing feelings.

A comparison that may help you understand this is a woman's usual difficulty with sexual feelings. If, as a woman, you feel uncomfortable in expressing your sexual feelings, you can better understand how many men feel about feelings in general. If, as a man, you feel awkward and embarrassed when you try to verbalize your emotions, you can appreciate how many women feel when they try to express themselves sexually.

Expressing feelings is not difficult only for men, however. There are many people, male and female, who grew up in nonexpressive families. They have no role model for communicating feelings and are likely to think of it as nonsense at best, and weak at worst. Our culture teaches us not to have feelings, not to express the ones we have, not to let them be known, to suppress them if we can. "Don't cry," "Cheer up," "Keep smiling," and "Be brave" are statements we can all remember.

Because many of us have learned to repress our

feelings, often without being conscious of it, we may be carrying around a "gunnysack" of compressed feelings that can burst open at any time.

Again—your spouse will never get to know who you really are unless you share your feelings. Many of us are actually strangers to our spouses. We cannot read interiors by looking at exteriors. Feelings define the essence of a person. A person cannot be known until that person's feelings are known. If you share only thoughts, opinions, facts, you might as well be sharing a book you've read. It is only when you can share your pain, your loneliness, your fear, or your joy that you can have a deep, human, and real relationship.

The first step is to give yourself permission to have your feelings. Tell yourself over and over: "Whatever I am feeling right now is all right for me to feel, even if I don't like it and even if others think I shouldn't feel this way. This is how I'm feeling right now. Because it exists it's OK. I do not have to evaluate whether it is good or bad. It simply is, and I accept its existence."

When you give yourself permission to have your feelings, you fear them less and will be more able to share them with your spouse.

Unfortunately, many people have little language for identifying or listening to feelings. The following lists contain words in two categories: when your wants and needs are being met, and when they are not. Underline all the feelings that you have felt during your marriage. Now go back and check the feelings you can visualize yourself feeling and expressing. Discuss with your spouse when and why you felt that way. Then discuss feelings you would like to feel or feelings that would be very uncomfortable. Go over the list with your spouse again and again until you feel totally comfortable discussing yourself and your feelings with your spouse.

When Wants and Needs are Being Met

absorbed	excited	mellow
affectionate	exhilarated	merry
alive	expansive	optimistic
amused	fascinated	overwhelmed
appreciative	friendly	peaceful
astonished	fulfilled	proud
breathless	glowing	radiant
calm	good humored	refreshed
cheerful	grateful	relieved
complacent	helpful	secure
confident	inquisitive	spellbound
curious	inspired	stimulated
delighted	intense	surprised
eager	interested	thrilled
elated	invigorated	trusting
encouraged	jubilant	wide awake
engrossed	keyed up	zestful
enthusiastic		

When Wants and Needs Are Not Being Met

afraid	depressed	gloomy
agitated	detached	guilty
aloof	discouraged	hateful
angry	disgusted	helpless

anxious	disheartened	hesitant
apprehensive	dismayed	horrible
beat	downcast	hostile
blah	edgy	hurt
bored	embarrassed	infuriated
cold	exasperated	insecure
confused	fatigued	irked
cross	frightened	jealous
dejected	furious	jittery
let down	passive	sleepy
listless	perplexed	spiritless
lonely	provoked	startled
mean	resentful	suspicious
miserable	scared	thwarted
nervous	shaky	troubled
nettled	skeptical	uneasy

The next step involves learning to share your feelings with your spouse on a daily basis. The easiest way to do this in the beginning is in a letter, because your spouse will not be there to inhibit you in any way with looks, comments, questions, and nonverbal behavior.

Assignment

So each of you now take ten or fifteen minutes, go someplace quiet, and write a letter to your partner. Let the letter describe how you are feeling about your relationship right now. There are two guidelines for this. The first is to make sure you are telling how you feel, which is an internal state like those described in the above list of words, not how you think. "I feel like you don't love me," is not a feeling; it's a thought. "I feel hurt because you won't talk with me" is a legitimate feeling.

Another guideline is to describe your feelings in mental images, rather than just words. The plain truth is that we don't have enough vocabulary for our feelings. "I feel hurt" doesn't give you a lot of information. There are many ways we can feel pain. "I feel like a knife is going through my heart" lets you know exactly what it's like. We would therefore like you to use images, analogies, and metaphors. Describe the feelings in colors, where they affect your body, how an animal or a child in a certain situation might feel that way, or when you've felt that way before. Your goal is to get your spouse to understand or feel what you are feeling, and any means you can use to accomplish this is good.

After you have written your letters, come together, exchange them, and discuss them for ten or fifteen minutes. Here again, there are very specific guidelines. The person reading the letter has only one task—to understand or feel what his/her spouse is feeling. Thus two things are forbidden. You must not indicate in any way that your spouse "shouldn't" feel that way. Remember, feelings are neither right nor wrong; they just *are*. Everyone has a right to feel the way he/she is feeling! Second, you must not start giving advice or start trying to solve the problem. That will come later. At this point it will just sabotage the expression of feeling. The listener's job is setting up a safe environment for the other to speak. You must make it safe! This is critical. If you start giving advice or discounting feelings when your partner shares with you, you are very carefully conditioning him/her not to be open and real with you. If you're honest you will recognize that as a major reason why couples do not level with each other; they've learned not to!

As you read your spouse's letter you may ask questions and seek clarification until you can experience what he/she is feeling. A good way to do this is to describe how you imagine it is to feel that way and ask if it's like that. Other questions you can ask are: "How does your feeling make you feel physically?" "Are any other feelings associated with this one?" "Have you ever felt this way before? When?" "What makes the feeling worse? What makes it better?" When you are confident that you understand your spouse's feelings and have communicated that to your spouse, you change roles and let your spouse ask you about the feelings in your letter. Do not spend more than ten or fifteen minutes exploring these feelings. If you do, you will be tempted to move into solving the problem. Do this daily for at least a week before you go on with this book. You will be amazed how much you will grow in the understanding of your partner.

Pick out a topic daily that you would like to explore your feelings on. Possibilities include: (1) How do I feel about our sex life? (2) How do I feel about money (or the children, in-laws, job, etc.)? (3) How do I feel about death? (4) What feeling do I have the most difficulty expressing? (5) What feeling do I have that I think is the most difficult for you to understand? (6) How do I feel when I have hurt you?

The list is as long as your imagination! Write the

letters when you are alone and quiet, then share them together at the end of the day. Do this for at least a week before moving on to the next section.

ACTIVE LISTENING

> *I know that you believe you understand what you think I said, but I am not sure you realize what you heard is not what I meant.*
>
> —Anonymous

Communication, in a nutshell, means message sent equals message received. If the message isn't received, no communication has taken place. Communication, therefore, begins and ends with listening. You always sense when your spouse has stopped listening, right? You know you do! Well, your spouse also senses when you've stopped listening. And communication stops if listening stops!

The main thing that gets in the way of effective listening, according to the experts, is our tendency to evaluate. We all tend to judge, to evaluate, to approve or disapprove the statements or opinions of another person. This tendency is even stronger with married couples because of the strong emotions involved. The stronger our feelings and emotions are, the more likely we are to evaluate and judge.

If having a tendency to evaluate takes away from

effective listening, then it's logical that we must try to listen nonevaluatively. This means listening to the other person's ideas as they are expressed in an effort to understand them, not judge them. This ability to put yourself in another person's position, to see the situation as the other is seeing it, and to experience what the other is experiencing, is called "empathy." Thus, empathy is critical to good communication and is expressed through a technique known as "Active Listening."

Listening doesn't mean just sitting still with your mouth shut. (Although holding your tongue can sometimes be a large part of it. Try it!) Rather, listening is an active process in which you also participate. Active listening is stating in your own words what you think your spouse just said and how he/she is feeling. That's all! It can also be called "paraphrasing," "feeding back," "checking it out," or "reporting back." It is trying to understand what the sender is feeling or what the message means, and feeding it back for the sender's verification.

An example: Sender: "I can't believe that guy ran into my car and then said it was my fault." Receiver: "You seem really angry that he wrecked your car and then blamed you."

Some lead-ins for active listening are:

"What I hear you saying is . . ."

"Sounds like you . . ."

"In other words . . ."

"So how you felt was . . ."

"What happened was . . ."

"Do you mean . . ."

Simple, isn't it? And amazing that anything so simple can be so powerful. Active listening does not imply agreement. It only communicates, "I know where you're coming from." If you consistently use this skill in your marriage you will see the following things occurring:

1. We said the ability to get into your spouse's skin and view the world the way he/she views it is called empathy. There is no way for you to move to negotiating conflict unless you have empathy for your partner's position. (Indeed, you actually have no right to comment on your partner's worldview until you understand it.) Active listening greatly enhances your capacity for empathy.

2. Active listening implies being attentive to your spouse. When you're really attentive to each other, you pick up on things before they blossom into full-blown arguments. You learn to recognize quickly "where the other person is at!"

3. The absolute number one cause of communication problems in a relationship is a misunderstanding of the sender's message by the receiver when neither is aware the misunderstanding exists. John says something, Mary takes it another way, and neither ever knows it happened. Mary assumes John meant it the way she takes it, and John assumes Mary takes it the way he means it. Wars have been fought over this! Active listening automatically eliminates this possibility.

4. Active listening fosters a kind of catharsis or ventilation. Often negative feelings seem to disappear like magic after they are expressed and heard.

5. Active listening promotes warmth between married couples. Being heard and understood by an-

other person is immensely satisfying. Sometimes there's an explosion of joy and relief to finally have been heard by another person. A typical comment is, "Thank God he finally realized what I have been trying to say!"

6. Your spouse will be more willing to listen to your thoughts and ideas if you have listened to his/hers. Thus active listening facilitates problem solving instead of just complaining.

7. It helps you remember what was said!

Be forewarned: Active listening, though simple, is not easy. It does not come naturally. What comes naturally is responding to our partner's messages with advice giving, blaming, criticizing, interpreting, suggesting, teaching, preaching, judging, withdrawing, or even sympathizing. These are all ineffective ways of responding.

Another warning: Be prepared to find yourself changing. If you truly put yourself in your spouse's skin and see the world as he/she sees it, you run the risk of having your own world view changed. You never leave your home in the morning and return to it at night the same person; you're always changed by your experiences. Likewise, you'll never go into the world of your spouse and return the same person. People are changed by what they really understand. This can be scary—but beautiful. It's this kind of change that moves couples together.

Let's start practicing this skill now. You and your spouse will take turns giving a one-to-three sentence answer to the following questions:

1. What is one thing you like about your life right now?

2. What is one thing you dislike about your life right now?

3. What is one thing you like about your work?

4. What is one thing you dislike about your work?

5. What is something good that happened to you today?

6. What is something bad that happened to you today?

After one of you answers a question, the other gives a one-to-three sentence active-listening response to see if he/she understood the message. Do not evaluate or judge the message, just paraphrase it. *Remember to feed back feelings as well as meaning!* "You seem frustrated because your job is so confining!" This is the most important part of active-listening. After each of you has gone through all six questions, gotten feedback, and feels comfortable with the skill, do the following exercise:

Assignment

The husband tells the wife something he believes she has never fully understood about him. All the husband has to do is talk, but the message must be about himself. The message must not be an attack on his wife (although he may express hurt or anger at a specific behavior of hers). The wife's job is to give an active-listening response at intervals to what's just been said. She will say what she has heard so far and find out if she is getting it right. Every time she does this, the husband decides whether she has really understood. He can make corrections in what she says and she builds those corrections into a new attempt at paraphrasing. A good rule of thumb in getting to your spouse's feelings is to put yourself in his/her place and see how you would feel. You keep going, with the husband talking and correcting, and the wife active-listening, until he is satisfied that he has been understood. The husband is the sole judge of whether understanding has taken place. You may be amazed at how long it takes, but keep at it until the husband is satisfied he has been heard. Then repeat the entire process, switching roles.

Let's listen in as Lee and Christy do this exercise:

Lee: The one thing I've never thought you really understood about me, Christy, is my need to be alone sometimes. It's a real, almost physical, need sometimes. You seem to take it as a rejection of you, but it has nothing to do with you. I just feel like I'll explode if I don't get away; I get itchy and antsy, and just need to be alone.

Christy: You're saying, then, that there are definitely times when you don't want to be around me and that I should understand. Is that right?

Lee: Well, not exactly, because you said "around me." It's around anybody. When I get this way I don't want to be around you, or the kids, or our parents, or my friends, or my coworkers, or anybody.

Christy: OK, so you want to be totally alone when you feel this way, and it's nothing personal, right?

Lee: Right—but only when I'm feeling that way.

Christy: Then can you help me with how and why you "feel that way"? Do I cause it and can I do anything to help?

Lee: I don't know exactly what causes it. Maybe it's

just conditioning. I always had a lot of alone time as a child and teenager. Maybe I just got used to it.

Christy: What you mean, then, is because you were a loner as a kid means you've got to stay a loner now?

Lee: No, I wasn't a loner as a kid. I had lots of friends and participated in many activities. But because I was an only child I had a lot of quiet time by myself, and it was an important part of my life. I could think better then and work out my problems.

Christy: It wasn't excessive, then? Just good times when you could think through your problems?

Lee: That's right. And maybe it has something to do with problems. Maybe when I get under a lot of stress that's when I need some alone time.

Christy: So you've noticed when you have a lot on your mind that can be when you need to be alone?

Lee: Basically, yes, I think that's it.

Christy: Thank you, Lee, for sharing that, and I'll try to be more understanding in the future.

Your next assignment is to do this every night for a week before you go on with this book! Practice this skill well. It's the foundation for everything else that comes.

"I" MESSAGES

"Boy, you've really done it again! You made a real fool out of yourself last night! Why do you always drink so much and embarrass me like you do? You're a moron and a lush!"

What was the one word you noticed being used over and over in the message above? That's right—

"you." These messages are referred to as "you" messages because they make *you* the focus of responsibility. I deny any responsibility for my reactions. "You" messages lay a guilt trip on you. I put you in the position of being the bad guy. These messages are almost always accusatory and will almost certainly lead to defensiveness. However, you do have to send messages to your spouse, as well as receive them. There's more to communication than listening, even active listening. How can you send a message, especially if you are clearly upset and even have a right to be, without making your spouse defensive? The answer is with an "I" message. "I" messages are expressions of self-responsibility, thus placing ownership of the problem where it belongs. That is, I am assuming responsibility for my own reaction. I own my feeling. No one else is pulling my strings. The power is mine. I'm not saying "You make me mad," giving you the power to push my buttons. If I give an "I" message, I'm emphasizing that someone else may have reacted differently. I may not even understand my reaction, yet I know it has been the result of something in me.

It's important to add that messages that begin with "it" or "we" can be almost as negative as "you" messages. An "it" message is underresponsible. It implies that responsibility is somewhere else. It's difficult for the listener to respond, because the speaker denies participating in the problem. Example: "It really makes me mad when this happens."

On the other hand, "we" messages (which can include words like "everybody" or "all") are overly responsible. They speak for others. By definition the speaker is speaking not only for him/herself, but for the listener or others as well, something he/she just doesn't have the right to do. Example: "We all know how irritating that is."

An "I" message does not suggest that I must not mention "you." After all, if I am upset with something in my marriage, it has to concern my spouse. However, if I stick only with my spouse's behavior and its effect on me, I am less likely to create defensiveness. To repeat: an "I" message is a message in which the sender takes responsibility for his/her feelings and behavior and speaks only for him/herself—often beginning with the word "I." The "I" message generally describes the effect someone else's behavior has on the speaker. Some examples are:

"I am really hurt because you forgot my birthday."

"I am angry because you left your clothes all over the floor."

"I get upset when I'm being interrupted and can't get my ideas completely expressed."

An easy way to remember what an "I" message consists of is to remember the XYZ formula:

"When you do X
In situation Y
I feel Z"

There are many advantages of using "I" messages:
—An "I" message is much less apt to provoke resistance, defensiveness, or rebellion. Because it deals only with behavior, it is not a put-down. It

doesn't suggest there is something bad about the person because he/she engaged in that behavior.

—People often don't realize the effect their behavior has on their spouses. They are often willing to listen and change their behavior when this effect is made clear in a message that is not a put-down.

—"I" messages influence others to send similar honest messages whenever they have a feeling. "I" messages from one person in a relationship promote "I" messages from the other.

—The sender of an honest "I" message risks becoming known to the other as he/she really is when feelings are shared. As we have already discussed, the honesty and openness that come from sharing feelings foster intimacy.

Assignment

Before we practice these messages, take a moment and see if you can recognize an "I" message. Put a plus (+) beside any "I" message below and a minus (−) beside any "you" message.

__+__ 1. I get irritated when I'm constantly quizzed about where I've been.

__−__ 2. You idiot, you put all the papers in the wrong places.

__+__ 3. I feel you are inconsiderate and selfish to do that.

__−__ 4. I can't get my work done with you constantly talking to me.

__+__ 5. When you complimented me on my work I felt really great.

__−__ 6. How could you do such a dumb thing to me?

_____ 7. I think you should cut the grass before you go out.

_____ 8. I get upset when you use the car and bring it back on empty.

_____ 9. You are really terrible to treat me like this.

___+__10. I get lonesome and depressed when I'm left alone every weekend.

___+__11. You were an hour late, and I was afraid something had happened.

_____12. It's your fault I make mistakes because you watch me like a hawk.

Answers are given below.

_____

Statements 1, 4, 5, 8, 10 and 11 were the "I" messages (+). Did you miss 3 or 7? They are "you" messages disguised as "I" messages. "I feel you are inconsiderate" is the "you" message "you are inconsiderate" disguised as an "I" message. Did you miss 5 or 11? They are "I" messages that start with "you." An "I" messages does not have to start with "I"!

_____

There are four rules that you should keep in mind as you use these messages:

1. The messages should be direct. This means you don't assume people know what you feel, think, or want. Indirect communicators assume that others somehow know how they feel. They assume their spouses can read their minds. As a matter of fact, you should assume your spouse is a poor mind reader and hasn't the faintest idea of what you're thinking. Statements like "He knew I'd be upset if he did that" have no place in a marriage. Also, indi-

rect communicators sometimes know they need to communicate but are afraid to do so. These people resort to nonverbal communicating, hinting, or telling a third party (in hopes the spouse will get the message). These are all risky ways to communicate; the message could be ignored, misinterpreted, or simply not received.

2. The messages should be immediate. If you are hurt, angry, or otherwise upset, delaying communication will often make it worse. Anger and hurt can accumulate and fester, and explode later in harmful passive-aggressive ways. Sylvia is hurt because her husband forgot her birthday. She says nothing, but burns several dinners and refuses to make love for weeks. There are two additional reasons for airing your grievances right away: (1) When you establish a clear relationship between what your spouse does and its effect on you, you increase the likelihood that he/she will learn what you want or need and adjust his/her behavior accordingly. (2) Immediate communications are more exciting and increase the intimacy you're searching for.

3. The messages should be clear. A clear message doesn't leave things out and it isn't worded in fuzzy jargon. "I'm somewhat concerned about . . ." is not a good message when you're decidedly angry about something. Unclear messages open themselves up to a world of misinterpretation.

4. The messages should be straight. This means that what you are saying is the real purpose of the message. Hidden agendas, disguised intentions, and ulterior motives are manipulative and destroy intimacy. Ask yourself, "Is this really what I'm feeling?

What do I really want? Is this really what I want him to hear?" If your answers indicate you're not being honest, try again and state your real needs and feelings. Saying "I'm angry because you're playing golf again" when you're actually feeling hurt, unloved, and ignored is not being straight!

Practice now giving "I" messages to your spouse in the following situations:

1. Your spouse is openly flirting with your best friend.

2. Your spouse has written a check without recording it, which has overdrawn your back account.

3. Your spouse has just broken a tennis date with you to play with his/her best friend.

4. Your spouse is yelling at the children because of pressures at work.

Assignment

Now that you have role-played this skill, it's time to use it with real issues. Your assignment for the next few days is simply to give your spouse one honest, straightforward "I" message daily about something that's going on in your life. Your spouse does not need to respond (remember, the issues are still on the back burner) except to say, "I appreciate your leveling with me." Do this daily for at least a week. Again, you are making a habit of a skill that will be invaluable later!

CHAPTER 5

Advanced Communication Skills

*As friends, we don't see
eye to eye, but then we don't
hear ear to ear either.*

—Buster Keaton

Up until now we have been concerned with communication skills that each person can use independent of the other: You do not need your partner's cooperation. Now we will put these skills together with a technique in which both partners are actively involved.

THE ECHO GAME

It is called the "Echo Game," and is the most powerful tool yet for facilitating communication when a real problem or misunderstanding exists. Whenever you suspect that there could even possibly be a misunderstanding between you and your spouse, suggest that you play the Echo Game. In this game the listener must feed back (echo) the meaning of the speaker's message to the speaker's satisfaction before responding to the message. The Echo

Game is used when the listener wants to be sure he/she is understanding the speaker or when the speaker wants to be sure he/she is being understood. The goal is the same in either case: To make sure the message sent equals the message received! Both "I" messages and active listening are important in this process.

In the Echo Game one partner requests the game, gives a message, asks what was heard, gets the message back, verifies it, then asks for a response. The partner responds, asks what was heard, gets the message back, verifies it, then asks for a response. Let's listen in as Christy and Lee play the Echo Game.

Christy: Lee, I'd like to play the Echo Game.

Lee: OK, go ahead.

Christy: I get hurt when you continue to break tennis dates with me to play with your friends. It makes me think you don't care about me. What do you hear me saying?

Lee: I hear you saying it makes you mad when I break tennis dates with you. Is that right?

Christy: No, not mad, just hurt—my feelings are hurt. Now what do you hear me saying?

Lee: It hurts you when I break a tennis date?

Christy: Yes, that's correct. Would you like to respond to that?

Lee: Yes, I was unaware it hurts you. It's just that I need to play with better players occasionally in order to improve my game. What do you hear me saying?

Christy: You feel you need to play with players better than I am sometimes to better yourself? Is that right?

Lee: Yes, that's correct. Would you like to respond to that?

etc.

At this point you're probably objecting to the use of stilted phrases, "What do you hear me saying?" "Is that right?" "Would you like to respond to that?" Never mind! Granted, they are stilted, but they are only crutches. When you get used to feeding back to your partner what you heard him/her saying you won't need to use these words. The process will be automatic. In the meantime, however, the phrases force you to listen by forcing you to feed back to your partner what he/she said before you can respond. You will be amazed at the number of problems that will no longer be problems after you use this technique.

Remember, the number one cause of communication problems in a marriage is a misunderstanding of the sender's message by the receiver when neither is aware that the misunderstanding occurred. One way to eliminate this possibility is the Echo Game.

You need a cassette tape player to practice this skill. Think back to a recent discussion when you suspect there may have been a misunderstanding between you and your spouse. Use the Echo Game to discuss this issue, but tape the conversation. Either partner can request the Echo Game. After you have finished rewind the tape, play it back, and notice where you did or did not use the correct phrases. Where did you do well and where did the process break down? Switch off, let the other person start with another issue, and go through this process again. Continue to practice this daily, using any subject that is not on the back burner. Remember, you are not trying to solve any of your major problems yet! You might discuss how you are feeling about your progress as you are working through this book.

Assignment

Practice the Echo Game for at least a week before you go on with this book. This alone will move you quickly to a better relationship because it requires the active participation of both partners and assures that "message sent" is "message received."

OTHER HELPFUL MESSAGES

The skills we have talked about so far are helpful and positive. Before we move into problem solving, it's important to look at other kinds of messages that fall into the same basic category: messages that move us closer to our spouses, that facilitate problem solving, that work to get us what we want. Notice we didn't say "good" or "right." We don't want to label types of communication messages as "good" or "bad," "right" or "wrong," because all messages are human—even negative ones. We tend to respond defensively because it is human nature to be defensive. It's much better to think in terms of messages that help us get what we want (closer to spouse, a happier marriage) and those that don't. Those that help we will call "helpful." Those that don't, that hurt our goal to be closer to our spouses, we will call "hurtful."

The key point is to remember your goal. For instance, if I meet a mugger, it might be appropriate to use a hurtful message; I could care less whether we are "close." I only want to protect myself. Similarly, if you want to avoid sex with your spouse, use a hurtful message—it's appropriate! However, if you want to move closer to your spouse, helpful messages will work, and hurtful ones won't.

Assignment

We'd like you now to get a big piece of paper, poster board, or newsprint. Put "Helpful Messages" at the top of the chart. Write with a magic marker in fairly big letters. As you read through the following messages, write down the ones that you think you need to use more of in your marriage. If only one of you thinks you need it, it still goes on the chart.

1. "I Would Like . . ." Statements

This is a first cousin to the "I" messages just described. It tells your spouse what pleases you or what you want, when what you want is a specific behavior.

Examples: "I would like it if you would hold my hand when we are walking." "I would like to go to Mother's house this weekend." "I would like for you to fix the door when you get a chance, please."

These statements must be made clearly and directly, something married couples don't often do. Couples hide and disguise wants in hints, sweet requests, and suggestions. Then when their wants aren't met, out come accusations or manipulations. Couples want their spouses to satisfy their desires without having to ask. "If I have to ask for it, I don't want it" is an idealistic copout. Your wants are met to the extent that your wants are known! You must help your spouse know what pleases you, what makes you feel loved. Is it giving you a flower, watching TV with you, rubbing your back, doing household chores, taking the initiative sexually? Exactly what? You are responsible for communicating to your spouse what you would like. Mind reading has no place in a marriage!

Another advantage of an "I would like . . ." statement is that it forces you to figure out what you really want. This can be very important. Many times you can be vaguely dissatisfied with the way things are without coming to grips with what you want in their place.

"I would like . . ." statements should rarely use the words "I need." "Need" implies something necessary for survival, which sends the signal "You must do this for me" to your spouse. This might backfire. We often like to do things for our spouses out of desire, but rarely out of compulsion or obligation. And though you may have forgotten it, you'll find the word "please" can be very effective!

We understand the fear many people have in assertively asking for what they want, but you are in a no-lose situation. If you get what you want, that's great! Even if you don't, you will conquer your fear of asking by continuing to do it. Remember the advantages of having your behavior independent of your spouse's behavior?

2. Open-Ended Questions

An open-ended question is any question that can't

be answered in one or two words. It's a probing question that encourages the speaker to expand on an answer.

Examples: "What's been going on at your job lately?" "What are your thoughts about the party last night?"

The open-ended question shows an interest in the speaker, a willingness to listen, and a desire to communicate. The closed-ended question, one that can be answered in one or two words (and any question that can be answered with yes or no falls in that category), tends to cut off communication. Notice the difference in these two questions: "What kind of things happened to you today?" and "Did you have a good day?" Open-ended questions are especially good for couples who complain that "we never talk to each other."

3. Agreeing with Part of a Criticism

This skill, often called "fogging," will become important when we move into conflict negotiation. You pretend you are a "fog bank": Anything thrown goes through you instead of bouncing back. You refuse to argue by seeming to agree with part of the criticism—saying there may be some truth to it.

Examples: Jim: "If you weren't so sloppy and disorganized, you could get your work done." Mary: "Maybe I could be more organized, but I still would like some help with the house."

Jane: "You're not wearing that to the party, are you? You look awful." Tom: "I guess I could look better, but I prefer to be comfortable."

You refuse to become defensive. You refuse to

waste time arguing over matters that keep you from solving your problems. You say it's OK not to be perfect. You say "I do hear your criticism; you don't have to keep repeating it."

4. Asking for More Specific Criticism

This is another skill important to conflict negotiation. You ask for more information in the form of specific behaviors after being criticized.

Examples: Sue: You really are a slob. Bob: Exactly what is it I've done that wasn't neat?

Bill: How could you be so stupid? Sally: Could you tell me exactly when I've done something that was dumb?

The words "slob" and "stupid" don't give enough information to even think about negotiating this conflict. Asking for more specific criticism gets the attack to focus on more specific behaviors that can be changed. This can turn an argument into a productive conflict negotiation session.

5. Self-Disclosure

Self-disclosing statements reveal something private about oneself. For that reason they are very similar to the "I" messages and "I would like . . ." statements discussed earlier. They also include past experiences, fantasies, dreams, accomplishments, abilities, mistakes, embarrassments.

Example: "I was so embarrassed at lunch today! Of all times to forget my boss's name, it had to happen when we met my two best clients."

The beauty of self-disclosing statements is that they move you closer to a warm, intimate relationship. When I talk about things totally external to myself, I put up walls that are safe. This kind of communications often tends to distance people. Crawling out from behind these walls can be scary because they've protected me for so long. Yet when I let you know the real me, warts and all, it signals trust and caring. And of course the person who self-discloses will be more likely to get self-disclosure back, moving the relationship to a deeper, more meaningful, intimate level.

6. Quantifying Wants and Feelings

This little trick works wonders for communication and problem solving. You simply put your wants and feelings on a rating scale of 1 to 10.

Example: "I'd like to eat out tonight, but it's only about a 3 on a scale of 1 to 10." "I get really angry when you put me down in front of my family, and that's a 10 on a 10-point scale."

It's difficult for language to express degrees of feelings and desires. "I'm angry" doesn't let you know how angry I am. I might not even tell you when I'm angry because you might think I'm angrier than I am. Yet information about degrees of feelings and desires is vitally important when it comes to solving problems. Consider a couple discussing where to eat out. He: "I'd prefer to go to Hardee's tonight because I have so much work to do when we get home. That's about an 8 on a 10-point scale." She: "I had wanted to eat at Le Chateau and really dress up, but it's just about a 2 on the 10-point scale." Solving this problem becomes really easy.

7. Citing Specific Behaviors

We touched on this one before. Only by putting complaints, concerns or compliments in the language of specific behaviors will you be able to make changes in your marriage.

Example: "You don't kiss me good-bye in the morning any more. I really miss that."

If you call me inconsiderate I probably don't have a very good idea of what you want. If you ask me to call you when I'm going to be late, I know exactly what you want changed.

8. Asking for Feedback

Feedback is what happens when your spouse tells you his/her reaction to what you have just said. Most couples live in a feedback vacuum. They rarely ask for or get feedback. It's important to ask for this feedback.

Example: "This has been an exhausting spring. I'd really like to stay at home this year on our vacation. What is your reaction to that?"

Asking for feedback encourages your spouse to give an active-listening response (assurance that the message sent is the message received, or express his/her own opinions or feelings. It is especially useful for couples who avoid communicating on important issues or tend to use overlong statements.

9. "You Are Good" and "You Did Something Good" Statements

These messages are the valuing kinds of messages we discussed in chapter 3. The message is "I value you" or "I value what you've done." Whether we call them compliments, strokes, warm fuzzies, encouragement, reinforcers, or rewards the effect is the same: Couples feel better about themselves, better about each other, and better about the relationship. A rule of thumb is a positive to negative ratio of 5 to 1. That is, if you must criticize your partner once, try to find at least five positive things to comment on. If you get much below that ratio, self-esteem will suffer. When self-esteem suffers, so does the marriage!

10. Mutual Topic Finding

This is a way for one spouse to check the other's willingness to discuss a particular topic at a particular time. It gives the spouse the option whether to discuss the issue then, instead of presenting him/her with a surprise attack.

Examples: "I'd like to talk with you about the bills that came today. Would right after supper be a good time?" "I'd really like for us to spend more quality time together. Can we talk about that now?"

Sometimes spouses do not have the time or energy to talk about topics when their partners are ready. Or they need to prepare for what will obviously be a confrontation. Inherent in mutual topic finding, therefore, is each partner's right to ask for a postponement of the discussion until circumstances are more favorable. Mutual topic finding is just common courtesy!

11. "I Intend . . ." Statements

These statements let your partner know what your intentions are.

Examples: "I'm on the verge of exhaustion. I'm not going to the party tonight." "I'm sorry I spent so much money, and I don't intend to do that again."

"I intend . . ." statements, since they are made independently of the spouse, need to be made with care. They are often best reserved for issues that are very important to the person making them or of little critical importance to either spouse, because they imply that the issue isn't open for negotiation. "I intend to go to the beach on our vacation" is a statement that may evoke hostility, whereas "I intend to go fishing this morning while you are shopping" would not.

Generally, however, spouses don't communicate their intentions often enough. Are you guilty of this? If so, there are four possible reasons: (1) You don't know what your intentions are; (2) You know what they are, but either forget or don't think they're important enough to communicate; (3) You want to keep your intentions hidden from your spouse; or (4) You are so dependent on your spouse that you have no independent intentions. None of these four situations is desirable. Generally speaking, when you do know what you intend to do in a certain situation, communicate that intention to your spouse.

12. "Say-Ask" Statements

These statements always come in pairs. The first statement says how the speaker thinks or feels about something, and the second asks the listener how he/she thinks or feels.

Example: "I'm ready to go to bed now, Jim. Would you like to come with me?"

Using say-ask statements avoids setting up the listener in a "damned if I do, and damned if I don't" situation. Think of the alternatives. If the wife asks Jim if he is ready to go to bed without stating her intentions, "no" could be interpreted as a sexual rejection, and a "yes" as retreating from her or avoiding her by going to bed early!

13. "Two-at-a-Time" Questions

These are when one question is followed up by another before the speaker responds with a message of his/her own.

Example: He: "What did you do today?" She: "Not a whole lot. Just got some reading done." He: "Oh? What did you read that was interesting?"

Like say-ask statements, two-at-a-time questions keep you from using the answer as a setup for an attack. Notice the difference in the exchange below:

Example: He: "What did you do today?" She: "Not a whole lot. Just got some reading done." He: "I figured you wouldn't get the grass cut."

Two-at-a-time questions also express the speaker's interest in the spouse's response. Notice the obvious disinterest in this speaker:

He: "What did you do today?" She: "Not a whole lot. Just got some reading done." He: "I didn't get anything done either. I'm really spinning my wheels."

We go back to listening here. Words are spoken at the rate of 125 to 175 per minute. Our ability to hear and understand words is four times faster than that! How do you use this time? Are you rehearsing what you're going to say the next time you get a chance? Or are you truly listening for meaning and feelings behind the speaker's words? Asking two questions at a time demonstrates a commitment to truly listen.

14. "How" Questions

These are questions that begin with the word "how." Using this word immediately lends a problem-solving orientation to the conversation.

Example: "How are we going to pay for our vacation?"

"Why" questions, on the other hand, usually have an accusatory tone. Rarely does the listener really want to know the reason why. Furthermore, the question usually leads to rationalization instead of problem solving. If you ask your spouse "Why in the world did you buy those clothes?" you are really saying "I don't want you to buy those clothes." All you'll get are rationalizations for buying the clothes!

Now that you have the list of messages that you need to work on, take the sheet and tape it to a wall in your bedroom. The list will remind you daily to put more of these messages into your communication. Practice these for at least a week before going on with this book.

You might also write the ones you need to work on the most on separate note cards. Keep these in view during your discussions. They will be excellent reminders.

CHAPTER 6

Negotiating Conflict

The reason you don't understand
me, Edith, is because I'm talking
to you in English, and you're
listening in dingbat!

—Archie Bunker

HURTFUL MESSAGES

Now that you are comfortable using positive kinds of communication, we are going to discuss the kinds of messages that you want to avoid if you want to improve your marriage. Again, these messages are normal and human, but they will never move you closer to solving your problems. Conflict is unavoidable, but there are fair ways of handling it and unfair ways of handling it. Some counselors refer to these as fair-fighting techniques and dirty-fighting techniques. We call the dirty-fighting techniques "hurtful messages" because they virtually always hurt your marriage. Remember, we're not saying these messages are "bad," we're only saying they don't work. They damage the relationship, hurt self-esteem, and produce defensiveness, resentment, resistance, and antagonism. So if your goal is to solve your problems and have a happier marriage, you must stay away from these messages.

Assignment

Again, get a large piece of paper, poster board, or newsprint and a magic marker. As you read through the following messages, write down any that you remember having heard during your marriage. It's going to be a long list, so go over the list slowly and discuss it with your partner. You will probably need more than one sheet of paper.

1. Hitting Below the Belt

Everyone has a psychological belt line, below which they are vulnerable and where attacks are foul. You have no more right to hit your spouse below the belt than does a boxer! Example: "How can you expect to get a good job as fat as you are?"

I have a right to set my own belt line. No one else can really know what is especially painful to me. However, if I set my belt line up around my neck (virtually anything you say to me is "off limits"), I am also fighting dirty!

2. The Achilles Heel

The Achilles heel is the one spot that is the most sensitive. Attacking that spot is dirty fighting at its worst.

Example: "The only reason you want a baby now is because of the abortion you had when you were sixteen."

3. Garbage Collecting

This is continually bringing up irrelevant past garbage. It can also be called the "psychiatric museum." Example: "You've never liked my parents. I'll never forget how rude you were to Mother the Christmas we lived in the old house."

Are you the one who says, "Remember on January 12, 19— when you . . . ?" (It's now six years later.) If so, remember, ancient history belongs in a history book! A good rule of thumb is, "never go back past now."

4. The "Kitchen-Sink" Fight

This is a fight where everything is thrown in but the kitchen sink! This is probably the most common hurtful tactic that couples use. If you can get into the habit of discussing only one issue at a time, no exceptions, you are well on your way to negotiating conflict.

Example: He: "Look at these bills! You've got to stop spending so much money." She: "If you made a halfway decent salary it wouldn't be a problem. Don't you have any ambition?" He: "Get off my back about my job. You sound like your mother— nag, nag, nag!" She: "My mother? It just happens to be your mother that is always sticking her nose in our affairs!"

5. Hit and Run

This is often called "getting the last word in first." It is any statement or action that cuts off communication before the problem is solved.

Example: "If that's the way you feel about me, then just forget it. I'm leaving!"

6. Gunnysacking

This is storing grievances away in a mental gunnysack until it finally bursts open and spills everything out. Gunnysacking results from the inability to be assertive about wants, needs, and feelings. It is very common and always leads to problems.

7. Overkill

This is the result of gunnysacking. The response is inappropriate to the stimulus. Measure your weapons against the seriousness of the issue. Nuclear bombs shouldn't be used on pea-shooter causes.

8. Monologing

This is not letting your partner get a word in edgewise. As a rule of thumb, any message that takes more than a minute without giving the other person a chance to respond is probably too long.

9. Interrupting

The hidden message here is obvious: "I don't need to listen to you. Your message couldn't possibly be important."

10. Passive-Aggressive Techniques

These are any techniques that appear passive, but are actually aggressive. Silence (feeling resentment, anger, hurt, etc., without verbalizing it) is the most dangerous. "Silent sulking" is a dirty and deadly weapon. Staying away from home or forgetting are also passive-aggressive.

11. Character Analysis/Labeling

These statements imply a helpless basic flaw. "You're so neurotic." "What a slob you are."

Stupid, selfish, ugly, evil, asinine, mean, disgusting, lazy and worthless are examples of character analysis. They imply an indictment of the total person instead of a specific behavior.

12. Stereotyping

"That was a typical male chauvinist pig remark."

13. Mind Reading

This is when one spouse assumes what the other is feeling or thinking without asking. It is also called "crystal gazing."

Example: "I know you don't love me."

Mind reading can also involve ascribing motives —"You're just trying to make me mad"—or interpreting—"You are hostile to me because I remind you of your mother." Unless you received a crystal ball for a wedding present, you have no right to try to read your spouse's mind! Granted, this is human. If something worries or delights me, I assume it worries or delights you. I think you think like I think. But we cannot possibly know the intricate workings of another person's mind.

There is no one so like you, not even your spouse, that you can safely project your thoughts, feelings, or motives onto him or her.

14. Overgeneralizing

These are statements so broad they can't be verified.

Example: "Nothing I ever do is right for you."

"You're always . . ." and "you're never . . ." are the most common forms of overgeneralizing.

15. Put-Down Questions

These are rhetorical questions used to communicate dissatisfaction.

Example: "Why can't you be more responsible with money?" It's obvious the speaker doesn't want to know the reason why. He/she just wants the spouse to be more responsible with money!

16. "You Are Bad," "You Did Something Bad" Statements

These include any statements that imply the spouse or spouse's behavior is "bad."

Examples: "You acted like a fool at the party." "You're dishonest."

17. "You Should" Statements

"You shouldn't feel so bad." "You ought to be friendlier to my parents."

18. Defending Oneself

This is an attempt to prove that what you did was right or justified.

Example: "I was late only because I had to pick up your junk."

19. Sarcasm

This is making a witty comment, usually the opposite of what is meant, to express hostility. "Sure, you're never late. We really believe that one."

20. Commanding

This is directing in an authoritarian tone, implying no choice.

Examples: "Turn off that radio right now." "You can't do that in my house."

21. Threatening

Threats fall in many categories. They can be medical: "I'll have a heart attack"; mental: "You're driving me crazy"; suicidal: "I'll kill myself"; emotional: "I just won't care what you do"; sexual: "You can forget lovemaking if you go out tonight"; financial: "Try that again and there go your credit cards"; exposing: "Wait until Mother hears about this"; religious: "God will send you straight to hell for that"; or separating: "Pull that one more time and I'm leaving."

The message is always the same: "If you don't give in or change, the consequences will be bad!" Threats may work for short-term gains but they never improve a marriage.

22. Joking

This is turning the whole thing into a joke with a witty remark. The underlying message is, "You are not worth taking seriously."

23. Expressing Dissatisfaction through a Third Party

"Sorry we're late. Julie has never learned to keep appointments on time."

24. Changing the Subject

This is shifting topics in spite of signals that the other wants to discuss something.

Example: He: "I'm worried about our finances."

She: "Me, too. I hope my check comes soon. By the way, I saw Frank today and he . . ."

25. Ignoring

This is simply ignoring an important message of the other.

Example: He: "Oh, boy, what a day I've had today." She: "Did you remember to pick up the bread?"

26. Playing Lawyer

This is disputing versions of past events.

Example: "I did not say that!"

Unless you have it on video or audio tape you're not going to be able to prove it anyway. Also, nine out of ten times it won't help solve the problem. Remember, there is no judge or jury that is going to rule on who is right or who is wrong. Playing lawyer is wasted effort—bogging down in childish disputes instead of solving the problem.

27. Assuming

This is assuming that a perception is a reality without checking it out. Never make assumptions! Studies have shown that perception of reality is rarely reality. Check it out! Check it out!

28. Premature Advice

This is giving advice without first exploring the subject thoroughly.

Example: "I think you ought to resign if you're going to be treated like that."

29. Speaking for Your Spouse

This is speaking for your spouse when he/she is actually present.

Example: "Jim doesn't care for another drink."

Speaking for your spouse is patronizing and grandiose. At worst it is an insult, and at best it preempts the spouse's effort to define his/her own insights.

30. Blackmailing

"You're giving me a headache (heart attack, depression etc.)."

31. Acting Out Anger

This is hitting, throwing something, getting drunk, etc. It is using behavior rather than words to express your anger.

32. Physical Abuse

This is when one spouse actually slaps, hits, pushes, shoves, or beats the other—any physical contact!

It is the dirtiest fighting of all! If you are being physically abused or are physically abusing your spouse, you *must* get professional help.

Assignment

Well, quite a list, isn't it? You probably have several sheets filled up by now. Your first task is to do what you did before: Tape the sheets to the wall in your bedroom so you will be constantly reminded of them. But this time you will go one step further. You must be aware and conscious of your use of these messages if you want to stop using them. You can't change behavior you don't recognize! Get out your cassette tape recorder again, put in a blank tape, and role-play a fight with your spouse. Role-play a subject that is not actually a problem in your marriage. For instance, if the husband is very shy around women, you can role-play a situation in which he flirted with every woman at a party the night before. With the recorder going, have an argument about that subject, using every hurtful technique you possibly can. Communicate in the absolute worst way possible. That tape player must run for at least ten minutes. After you finish, tell your partner the hurtful messages you noticed that he/she used. Then rewind the tape, play it back, and stop it to identify each hurtful message as it occurs.

What did you discover? Did you use some types of hurtful messages more than others? Did you use some that your spouse noticed that you were not even aware you used? Were you able to pick up on your spouse's negative messages? Did you always agree on whether a message was a hurtful one? If not, go back to the definitions and examples and discuss them until you agree.

Do this exercise every day for a week, always using a made-up situation. If you try it with a real problem in your marriage, you may generate hostility and defensiveness. Your goal at this point is simply to become aware of these hurtful messages and when you use them. Again—awareness is the key for prevention.

THE FAIR FIGHTING PROCESS

Now that you understand the kinds of messages that help and hurt in your marriage, we will show you how to negotiate conflict healthfully. First, let's clear up some misconceptions about marital conflict. For starters, conflict is absolutely inevitable! In even the very best of marriages, there will always be conflict. It could not be otherwise. Marriages are composed of two human beings, and two human beings will always have conflicting needs and desires. There are no two human beings exactly alike anywhere in the world! If you believe your marriage should never have conflict, you're automatically setting yourself up for disappointment. As a matter of fact, we have been oversold on the importance of "compatibility." Compatibility is probably a myth. There are too many ways a couple can be incompatible to ever achieve compatibility. Both might prefer the same kinds of activities, but one might be a "Morning" person and the other a "night" person. If both are night people, one might be shy and one outgoing. If both are outgoing, one might be a tightwad and the other a spendthrift. If both agree on money, one might be "laid back" and the other "uptight." And on and on and on. There is no limit to the ways couples can be compatible or incompatible.

Fortunately, although conflict is inevitable, it is also desirable! A totally stable marriage is like a totally stable person—pretty dull and boring. A conflict-free marriage is a devitalized one: It lacks passion and excitement. Lack of open disagreement usually means one of two things: (1) The couple simply doesn't care enough any more even to disagree; they are emotionally detached; (2) Instead of openly disagreeing, they fight covertly; they undermine each other without being open and honest. Conflict, therefore, is to be welcomed. Conflict can shake the status quo. Conflict can expose unrealistic expectations. Conflict can and does lead to change and growth.

If a happy marriage does not depend on the absence or presence of conflict, what does it depend on? The answer is the ability to negotiate the conflict to the satisfaction of both parties! Indeed, recent studies indicate that happy and unhappy couples have the same number of problems and the same problems! What determines marital satisfaction is not compatibility, but how the couple deals with the incompatibilities.

Almost all couples have trouble in negotiating conflict. One reason is that few of us have had effective role models for resolving conflicts. Even if we have learned good communications skills or how to nurture a marriage from our parents, we have seldom learned how to fight. There's an unwritten law in our culture: "Don't fight in front of the children." And parents who do fight in front of the children are rarely positive role models. They probably fight with attacking, aggressive techniques, or passive, nonassertive ones—neither of which work.

Fair Fighting Rules

Before we discuss how to fight fair, we need to review the "rules" that govern a fair fight.

1. Fight by appointment only. Decide together on a time and place to discuss the issue. No "Pearl Harbors" (surprise attacks) allowed!

2. Each person has the right to say "no," say "yes," to make a counter offer, to ask for more time or information.

3. Avoid all hurtful fighting techniques. Point them out to your spouse in a non-judgmental way when they occur. If you are the victim of really dirty fighting, shout foul!

4. Nip anger in the bud. If you become extremely angry, disengage from the argument and continue it at another time. This is not being a "fight phobic." It is plain common sense. If you're really angry you are much more likely to say things you don't mean.

Likewise, back off it you've struck a raw nerve in your spouse. Signs of extreme hurt or anger in your spouse should be a red flag telling you to pull back. Try again in a few days when he/she may be less sensitive. The future of your marriage doesn't rest on being able to resolve every argument right now. The future of your marriage rests on the confidence that there will be a future. Give yourself and your partner a cooling-down time.

5. Decide on your own ground rules. Some ground rules other couples have used are: (1) No fighting when drinking alcohol; (2) No fighting in front of the children; (3) No fighting with the TV on; (4) No swearing; and (5) No fighting when exhausted or hungry. Only you will know what ground rules make sense for you. But once made, these rules must not be broken!

6. Continually use "active listening" (checking it out, reporting back, paraphrasing both the content and the feelings) and "I" messages (I feel . . . when you . . .).

7. Discuss only one issue at a time! The only exception to this is when you suspect the real issue is not the one you are fighting over. Then try to surface the real issue. Real issues are often power, prestige, self-esteem, or personal "space" or freedom. We will talk more about real issues later.

8. There must be two winners. There is never a single winner in an honest intimate fight. Both either win more intimacy, or lose it. A bad argument is one where there is a winner and a loser. One partner will feel victorious, but the other will feel humiliated. One way or another, the loser will "get the winner back!"

THE TWO-STAGE PROCESS

Think of conflict negotiation as a two-stage process. Simply stated these stages are: Stage 1—Exploring the Problem; and Stage 2—Solving the Problem. Keep these stages distinct, because Stage 2 can contaminate Stage 1 if Stage 1 is not complete. If you try to solve the problem before you fully explore it, you sabotage yourself. Trying to solve the problem before it is fully explored can prevent you from solving it! Don't try to accomplish the two stages at the same time in the beginning. If, therefore, you have made an appointment to explore a problem one evening, make another one to try to solve it the next day.

Then if one of you starts to say something like "Why don't we do . . ." the other can come right back with "Hold on. That's not our job tonight. We're just examining all aspects of the problem now."

Stage 1—Exploring the Problem

Stage 1 consists of three components. We will discuss each of the three separately. They are: (1) Defining the problem, (2) Examining Multiple Viewpoints, (3) Validation.

DEFINING THE PROBLEM

This may seem to be unimportant, but it is actually a critical first step. You must agree on exactly what the problem is. You are not agreeing on the solution, only on what is the actual issue. If you don't define the problem, you may get side-tracked, or each of you might argue about a different problem.

EXAMINING MULTIPLE VIEWPOINTS

This is actually the heart of Stage 1. You need to examine your problem repeatedly from many angles and points of view until it is thoroughly understood by both parties. Compare it to examining a statue. If you view a statue only from the front at a distance of twenty-five feet you will have little true knowledge of its nature. Talking or writing meaningfully about it is impossible. You don't even have the right to try. But if you view the statue from all angles, distances and heights, that's a different story. You look at it in the sunlight and even the moonlight. Your understanding of the statue is now much greater and you are able to (and have the right to) talk or write about it meaningfully.

Similarly, the problems in a marriage must be examined from multiple viewpoints—from all angles and points of view. And you really don't have the right to try to solve the problem until this is done.

The multiple viewpoints in a marital conflict include:

1. The wife's needs and wants.
2. The wife's feelings, especially fears.
3. The wife's values.
4. The wife's current life situation.
5. The wife's past life situation that left her vulnerable to certain problems.
6. The husband's needs and wants.
7. The husband's feelings, especially fears.
8. The husband's values.
9. The husband's current life situation.
10. The husband's past life situation that left him vulnerable to certain problems.
11. Social and economic pressure on one or both partners.
12. Vocational pressures on one or both partners.
13. Physical or emotional illnesses that are affecting one or both partners.
14. The impact of their children on the marital partners.
15. Any additional information that might affect the problem.

The list might sound formidable, but it isn't. After a while it comes naturally. Use this list to begin with, but soon you will discover that the multiple viewpoints are automatic. After all the relevant information and viewpoints are out on the table and examined, you are ready for the next step.

VALIDATION

To this point, the process has maybe been long, but it hasn't been difficult. It is usually not hard to get multiple viewpoints out on the table. But now you must validate your spouse's position, and this can be hard to do. Validation means that you communicate to your partner that if you were he or she, standing in his or her shoes, given his or her background, values, needs, and feelings, that it would be reasonable to feel that way! You are not saying "I agree with you" or "You are right." You are only saying "It makes sense for you to feel this way, knowing what I know about you." You cannot communicate this reasonableness unless you feel it. And you cannot feel it unless you get in your spouse's shoes and see for yourself how reasonable it is for him/her to feel that way.

The importance of validation cannot be overemphasized. You do not have the right to try to solve a problem until you truly understand—not agree with —your spouse's position. Multiple viewpoints without validation will do nothing. What you must remember is that your spouse's views make sense to him or her, so if they don't to you, your knowledge is incomplete. Everyone operates from his/her own system of logic. Even a paranoid schizophrenic has a system of logic. You might not see it, but it's there. Your task is to discover your spouse's system of logic.

Empathy is the ability to put yourself in another

person's position and see the situation as the other is seeing it. The catch here is that you cannot walk in another person's shoes until you take off your own! To experience empathy you must get out of yourself. So leave all your preconceived ideas and values behind as you try to understand your spouse.

Listening skills are obviously critical here. If you are having trouble with validation, go back to the sections on active listening and sharing feelings. You may need to keep on asking your spouse to help you understand his/her position. If you're really stuck, try sleeping on it. You might wake up in the morning with more insight into your spouse's world.

When you are able to say to your spouse, "I understand your position. Knowing you, it is reasonable and makes sense for you to feel that way," then you have finished Stage 1, and you can move on to Stage 2, Solving the Problem.

Stage 2—Solving the Problem

Are you ready for the good news? The hardest part is now over. That's right! If you have successfully accomplished Stage 1—Exploring the Problem, you will be surprised at how easily the rest of it goes. It's amazing how solutions just seem to present themselves once you truly understand your spouse. It's like a jigsaw puzzle. Like a piece of a puzzle, each piece of information that has come out is probably meaningless by itself. But as more and more pieces fit together, the picture gradually emerges.

Remember the following guidelines when going into Stage 2—Solving the Problem.

1. The first order of business is to get yourselves into a problem-solving mindset. This means you have started thinking, "What we are about now is to solve the problem." If this does not occur you will stay in an endless circular argument.

2. The most important point is: Do not attack! Attacking your spouse will always lead you away from problem-solving rather than toward it. Think of your spouse as an army. If an army is attacked by the enemy, it has three options: (1) counterattack, (2) defend, or (3) retreat. Your spouse will also use one of these three options when attacked. He or she will get defensive, launch a counterattack, or withdraw! None of these options will move you toward solving the problem. Thus, the number one rule is *Do not attack!*

3. Constantly ask yourself and your spouse, "What is reasonable?" The word reasonable should always be foremost in your mind. Do not ask for or expect unreasonable results. If you are married to a man who is 5'5" and weights 200 pounds, it is reasonable to expect him to lose 10 pounds. It is not reasonable to expect him to grow three inches. While this is clearly a ridiculous example, we often expect changes from our partner as unreasonable as a growth spurt.

4. Be wary of compromise. Compromise is highly touted, but it can be manipulative. You only need to remind yourself of labor unions or professional athletes to realize that someone faced with compromise is apt to inflate his/her starting position. This is clearly not being open, honest, or real. If no other alternatives exist compromise may be unavoidable,

but remember that in a compromise neither party wins. Both have to give in to reach a compromise. Truly effective conflict negotiation results in "win-win," not "win-lose" or the "lose-lose" of compromise.

5. Remember that you can't put all responsibility for change on the other. The "take it or leave it" philosophy is not only unfair, it will backfire. If you want a change in your relationship, you will have to change!

6. Start from "I would like . . ." and go from there. This forces you to get away from nebulous negatives and move to specific positives. A nebulous negative is "You never communicate with me." A specific positive is "I would like for you to talk with me fifteen minutes a day."

7. Avoid scorekeeping: "I did three things for you; you only did two for me." This is petty and irrelevant. The value of behavior rarely depends on how often it occurs.

8. Identify areas of agreement before suggesting change. Most couples have many more similarities and compatibilities than differences. Remind yourself that your relationship is greater than the issue you're fighting about. Focusing on the areas of agreement will often make the areas of disagreement seem more manageable.

9. A gold star goes to the first one who introduces one of the "Big Three." Any of these three techniques immediately moves the focus of the discussion from complaining to solutions. They are:

1. The question, "What can we do to make things better?" Memorize this question and use it often. It

is truly powerful. It will immediately catapult you out of deadlocks. If your spouse asks you this question, reply with what you would be willing to do to make things better. It is extremely difficult to respond to this question in a defensive or attacking manner.

2. Bargaining. When making a bargaining statement, the speaker offers to do something for the spouse if the spouse does something in return. Example: "Let's make a deal. If you go to the ball game with me tonight, I'll go visit your parents next weekend." Even if your spouse doesn't take you up on your bargain you've moved into a problem-solving mindset. There will probably be a counterproposal. Bargaining is the perfect example of the advantage of offering positive rather than negative incentives. "If you do what I want, I'll reward you" is much more effective than "I will punish you if you don't."

3. Listing options and choosing among them. This is the most complicated technique but probably the one that you will need to use for really serious problems. Here again, the one who says something like, "Why don't we make a list of all the options we have?" gets the gold star. The idea is to generate as many options as possible, even wild, off-the-wall ones, before any are evaluated. Both partners think of as many creative solutions to the problem as possible—even clearly ridiculous ones. This is beneficial for two reasons. An off-the-wall solution may give rise to one that will work. Creativity begets creativity. Also, both partners are thinking of solutions rather than pushing their solutions. This avoids the sense of one person winning and one person losing.

Both are trying to figure out a solution acceptable to both. Both have won when this happens, and neither has won until it does!

Listing options must be kept separate from evaluating them, or fewer options will be brought up. If an idea is rejected or ridiculed when it is presented, the presenter won't want to think of any more options. The habit of evaluating an idea when it is presented is very strong. Try your best to overcome it.

After all the options have been listed, the next step is simply to pick one and try it. If all the previous steps have been successful, the best solution often just seems to present itself. The important point is that you pick an option and *try it!* You are not setting anything in concrete or trying to solve the problem for life. If both partners realize they have the option to come back and say, "Hey, this isn't working. Let's talk about it some more," they will be more likely to agree to a solution. This is actually the last step. After a solution is agreed upon and tried, at some point you will want to discuss it again. The questions to ask are, "Is this working?" "Can we both be happy with the way things are?" "Is the issue really actually settled?" If the answer to any of these questions is "no," start the whole process of listing options and choosing again. Continue until you find one that works—that is, both partners feel happy and at peace with the solution.

You will occasionally be truly deadlocked on a problem. There just doesn't appear to be any solution that will satisfy both husband and wife. The answer to this might be "experimental roles." Each partner agrees to the solution the other prefers for an experimental period of time, say one month each. At the end of the two months, take inventory and see where you need to go from there. Or a partner can agree to do what the other thinks he/she should do, regardless of whether he/she wants to, during the same experimental period of time. We think you can see the advantages of this. Solutions we don't originally agree with often seem to work once they're tried! At least the deadlock has been broken, and a future attempt at negotiation will be more likely to be successful.

REEXAMINATION OF PRIORITIES

In spite of everything you may be unable to find an acceptable solution. Try reexamining your priorities. Most couples have certain requirements for a marriage, the things that are necessary for the marriage to continue to exist. The priorities many couples list are (1) affectionate harmony, (2) no infidelity, (3) economic union, (4) children, (5) socially and culturally accepted behavior, and (6) being number one with mate. Make a list of the things that are absolutely necessary for you in a marriage and see if your marriage has them. If it does, try to concentrate on these things instead of on what you don't have. This often has the result of changing what was "necessary" to "necessary and sufficient."

CHAPTER 7

Advanced Conflict Negotiation

> *I understand a fury in your words, but not the words.*
>
> —Shakespeare, *Othello*

WHEN THE SPOUSE KEEPS ATTACKING OR DEFENDING

It would be naive to believe that everyone trying to negotiate a problem will magically use only positive helpful communication messages. Old habits die hard, and defensive, attacking behavior is often a result of many years of practice. There are, however, things you can do if your spouse keeps attacking or defending.

The main thing to remember is that it takes two to fight! If you refuse to get defensive or attack after your partner does, the conversation will eventually take a problem-solving turn. Again, start with a statement of what you would like, and end by moving into bargaining or listing options. The best techniques to use in the middle are active listening, agreeing with part of a criticism, and asking for more specific criticism. If you have forgotten these skills, go back and review chapter 2.

Let's take a look at Sue as she tries to get Tom back on track:

Sue: Tom, I'd like to buy a new vacuum cleaner tomorrow. Our old one is completely shot.

Tom: Oh, heavens, not again! Money, money, money! What do you think I am, a money tree?

Sue: You seem to be really worried about money right now.

Tom: You're absolutely right. How could I not be, married to a spendthrift like you?

Sue: Could you tell me specifically when I've spent a lot of money that wasn't necessary.

Tom: All the time, that's when! Especially on this house. Why does it have to stay so immaculate? You're a compulsive cleaner!

Sue: You're right. I do like a clean house. That's why I'd like to buy a vacuum cleaner. The old one can't be fixed.

Tom: There you go—just thinking about the house again. It's all you ever think about. You don't even know I exist any more.

Sue: It sounds to me like you think I don't spend enough time or energy with you. I guess I have been neglecting our relationship lately. Look, let's make a deal. I'll buy the vacuum cleaner tomorrow morning, then instead of cleaning, I'll pack a big picnic lunch. We can drive up in the mountains and have a picnic under the autumn leaves. How about it?

MARITAL SCRIPTS

Very soon you are going to begin to use this process to solve your own problems. There is only one last step. Take an honest look at how you believe your marriage should be. Then ask yourself if this is something you have carefully thought out, or something you have just absorbed, primarily from your parent's marriage. We are all taught and trained by our parents. We can't get away from it. We often don't know what it is we have been taught, yet we all repeat it.

We call our preconceived ideas about what a marriage should be a "marriage script." When you go to a play, you assume the actors are all working from the same script. When you get married you assume your spouse will have the same script for marriage you have. But this is rarely the case. Everyone gets married with already-formed ideas of what is involved in being a husband or wife—what values, behaviors, and roles are expected of you. This is your script for marriage, and your script is usually based on the marriage of your parents. Over and over again you try to turn your marriage into a carbon copy of your parents' marriage.

Even if your parents have given you a negative role model that you consciously reject, your marriage script will unconsciously and unexpectedly sneak up. Script messages are buried deep within you. Unfortunately, they are buried alive, not dead, and they continue to influence you and your marriage. Your script includes hundreds of items: how to fight, when to be affectionate, how to treat each other, who handles the money, who does the gardening, who takes out the garbage, who disciplines the children, who answers the telephone, who does the shopping, and on and on.

Your parents are the primary source of your script, but the messages can come from other sources also. You get your script from the region where you were born, the neighborhood where you played, the childhood games you played, the family tales you overheard, the schools you attended, the sports you played, the friends you made, the books you read, the God you believed in.

To see how scripts can continue through generations, consider the story of the newlyweds and the ham. The wife cuts the end off the ham before putting it in the oven. When the husband asks why she does this, she says, "I don't know. My mother always did it." The next Sunday they visit Mom and he asks why she cuts off the end of the ham before she cooks it. She replies, "I don't know. *My* mother always did it." At Christmas they visit Grandmom, and he asks the same question. She replies, "Oh, heavens, I'd forgotten about that. I never had a pan big enough to hold the whole ham."

It's now time to find out whether you're doing something only because "My mother always did it," and then determine whether it's still right for you. Like the newlywed who does have a big enough pan, you may find that some of your beliefs and behavior aren't appropriate to your situation.

In the appendix are two worksheets, one for the husband and one for the wife. At the left of the sheet is a list of topics that are important in a marriage. In the space provided, write what you think your mother and father might have said about those topics. It doesn't matter whether you actually heard them say anything about those things. Just think of what they *might* have said, knowing what you know about them. At the bottom is a space for adding script messages you have gotten from other family, friends, school, church, neighborhood, etc.

After you fill out your worksheet, compare it with your spouse's worksheet. These lists are the skeleton of your marital script. Discuss where they are matched and where they are mismatched. Often just noticing that a problem is a case of mismatched scripts goes a long way toward solving it. As you discuss these lists with your spouse, you will discover two things: (1) your spouse's behavior may suddenly make sense when you see his/her script; and (2) someone who doesn't share your script may completely misinterpret what you say and do.

A good example is Diane and Mark. Diane's father always fixed everything the minute it was broken. He never had to wait to be asked; he was Mr. Fix-it and he loved it. Anything from a loose hinge to the washing machine was magically and magnificently working the next day. Mark's father, on the other hand, was a wealthy and busy executive. His mother always called a service man when something broke down. Minor repairs were done either by her or by a carpenter who came by fairly regularly. Now that Diane and Mark are married, she waits for him to fix things. He can't understand why she doesn't get the broken things repaired. She begins to think of him as a spoiled, lazy, self-centered man, and he thinks of her as a whining, helpless nag. When it is finally pointed out to them that they have a case of mismatched scripts, the tasks are quickly negotiated. Once again, we see that a large part of conflict negotiation is just seeing the other person's point of view!

The point is that there is no obviously "right" or "wrong" way. Who does household repairs depends on interest, ability, time, and money, among other things. There is rarely a "right" or "wrong" way in any other area of marriage either. Couples often experience distress and anger because it doesn't occur to them that there is more than one way (the way they have grown up with!) to look at the situation.

Take a look at your own script and decide which of your script messages is not appropriate to your life and your world today. Then decide how you'd like to rewrite your script for yourself now. Even labeling your preconceived values and roles as a "script" suggests the ability to edit or rewrite it. Take another sheet of paper and rewrite all the messages according to the way you want to live your life. Again, share these with your spouse. Are they more similar now? Can you think of any way to get them more similar?

After you have thoroughly discussed your scripts with each other and have rewritten them according to your own values, you are ready to move into using the problem-solving process with your own problems. However, any time communication breaks down or you reach an impasse, ask yourself these questions: "Am I trying to recreate my parents' marriage? Am I acting this way (believing this) because my parents did? Do I expect my spouse to act a certain way (believe something) because my parent did? Does that make it right? What is the appropriate thing for us in this situation right now?''

The more clearly you understand how your attitudes and behavior are shaped by past experiences, the more control you have over these things today!

List any other script messages you may have gotten about these topics from other family members, friends, teachers, church, your race or ethnic background, or society's definition of masculine or feminine roles.

SOLVING YOUR OWN PROBLEMS

The time has come for you to start negotiating the problems and conflict in your marriage. Go to the box you designated as the "back burner" and get out the list of goals you have for your relationship. You prioritized those goals: number one for the most important to you, two for the next most important, and so on. Between the two of you, pick out a goal that is the least important to you, but still a concern. This is the problem area you will begin with. It's very important to pick the least important because you are least likely to get emotionally upset over this issue. Strong emotions such as anger, hurt, or fear will get in your way until you are comfortable with the process. Remember, it took years for your marriage to get into trouble; you are not going to solve all your problems overnight. After you have agreed on the topic, decide on a time and a place to begin Stage 1—Exploring the Problem. You must not go on to Stage 2 until the next day at the earliest. Remember, if you allow yourself to start solving the problem, there's a good chance you won't finish everything involved with exploring it. Stage 1 consists of: (1) defining the problem; (2) examining multiple viewpoints; (3) validation.

Take some paper to the meeting you have set up. As soon as you are together, each of you state in your own words how you define the problem. If there is a difference between your definitions, discuss it until you agree. When you agree on the definition of the problem, write it down. Writing it down will make sure you are both seeing the problem in the same way (not the solution, just the problem) and will keep you on course.

Now write down all the multiple viewpoints. Though you may not need to continue doing this, it will prevent you from overlooking any important points in the beginning. Put the following headings on several sheets of paper:

1. The wife's needs, wants, feelings, values
2. The wife's current life situation
3. The wife's past life situation that left her vulnerable to certain problems
4. The husband's needs, wants, feelings, values
5. The husband's current life situation
6. The husband's past life situation that left him vulnerable to certain problems
7. Social and economic pressures on one or both partners
8. Vocational pressures on one or both partners
9. Physical or emotional illnesses that are affecting one or both partners

10. The impact of the children

11. Any additional information that might affect the problem

As you discuss the problem, fill in the information in the appropriate places on the paper. *Use active listening responses to check out your understanding of your spouse's comments.* If, for instance, you are discussing where to spend your summer vacation, the husband might disclose one of his values by saying, "It's important to me to go somewhere where I can go fishing. It's the only thing I truly love to do, and I rarely have a chance during the rest of the year." The wife might respond with something like, "You're saying that fishing is the activity you value the most and you'd like to go somewhere where the fishing is good?" When the husband acknowledges that the wife got the message right, they write "fishing" down under the space headed "Husband's Values."

During this process one person often monopolizes the conversation or interrupts the spouse. If this is a problem in your marriage, get an index card and write "Floor" on it. Whoever is holding that card has the floor and can speak. When he/she finishes, he hands the floor to the spouse. You can only speak when you have the floor. If your spouse has the floor and you would like to speak, you have to ask for the floor. This simple technique quickly identifies who is interrupting and who is monopolizing the conversation. When you are both satisfied that all of the important information is on the table you can go to validation.

Remember, validation means that you communicate to your partner that, if you were he or she, standing in his or her shoes, given his or her background, values, needs, and feelings, that it would be reasonable to feel that way—it makes sense for him/her to feel that way. If you have trouble with validation go back and review chapter 3. Do not shortchange this step: it is critical. If you cannot validate your partner's position, keep asking him/her what has led him/her to that position. If you don't understand your spouse's position, your spouse still knows something you don't! When each of you is able to validate the other's viewpoint by communicating that the other's viewpoint makes sense, you are finished with Stage 1. Now make another appointment for the next day for Stage 2—Solving the Problem.

When you meet again, discuss the problem with an eye out for a solution. Go back over the guidelines on page 87. You can each start with what you would like to see happen. Try to move to one of the big three: (1) the question, "How can I make things better?"; (2) bargaining; or (3) listing options and choosing among them. When you've solved the problem, you may want to put it in "contract" form to guard against forgetting. Instructions for contracting are in the next chapter. In any event, give yourselves a reward for being successful. How about a movie, a night out, a backrub, a bottle of champagne? Whatever will be pleasurable for both of you will be good.

Now that you have successfully negotiated a low-level concern, you can slowly progress up your ladder of goals. They will probably be increasingly difficult to negotiate, but you should be increasingly able to solve them. Don't try to make changes too quickly. It is better not to try to solve more than one problem per week. If any of the problems don't present solutions or appear to be too emotionally charged to handle at this time, put them back on the back burner for a while. It's more important at this point to keep the good, warm feelings between you than to find an absolute answer to every problem. When you find yourself truly stuck, or recognize the same theme running through most of your problems, it's time to try to uncover the real issues in your marriage!

UNCOVERING THE REAL ISSUES

All marriage counselors know that the real issues you need to address may not be the ones you are fighting about. It stands to reason, therefore, that if you constantly fight over things that have a recurrent theme, or if you never solve problems once and for all, you need to pinpoint the real issues behind your fights. A good clue that there are deeper issues behind the surface issues is when the emotions of you or your spouse are out of proportion to the stimulus. If you or your spouse are more hurt, or more angry, than the situation calls for, dig a little deeper. Try to ask yourself four questions: (1) Why am I so upset about this? (2) What am I telling myself that means? (3) When else do I get so angry (hurt)? (4) Is there a common thread that runs through?

Take the case of Jennifer. Jennifer got angry, hurt, and depressed every time Jerry played golf on the weekend. After months of continually arguing over this, with no solution in sight, Jennifer analyzed why she was so upset. It wasn't because he played golf that often: he rarely played more than twice a month. The rest of the golf weekends and the entire weekends when he didn't play were spent with his family. It wasn't because he was loving or caring. In every other way he was a model husband. Jennifer was not a dependent, clinging wife. When Jerry was away during the week it didn't bother her. When Jennifer asked herself the four questions above she discovered that she interpreted golf as rejection, a rejection that meant that Jerry didn't love her. Jennifer remembered that her father, who openly rejected her, had often played golf on the weekends. Every time Jerry played golf, it triggered memories of her father's rejection.

If you look below the surface of an argument for a message that may be implied but not stated, you'll be well on your way to pinpointing the real issues. For example, arguments about in-laws are often actually about loyalty. The concern is really, "Who do you love more, your family or me?" Likewise, arguments about money often hide a deeper issue. Arguments may not be about money at all, but about whose interests are more important.

The real issues behind the surface issues often fall into four categories: (1) power, (2) rejection, (3) prestige, and (4) "space." Let's take each one separately.

Power

In our culture children are socialized to be competitive. Whether it is in school, sports, or with siblings, children learn early that it's better to win—to come out on top. By the time children become adults, they might *need* to win to feel good about themselves. It is necessary for their self-esteem. It becomes more important than relationships. When two people like this marry, every argument is just one more battle in the continuing war over "who is in charge of this marriage." But competition just does not work in a marriage. When one partner wins, the other loses. And the loser will "get the winner back." It will probably be in a passive-aggressive way such as silence, withdrawing, or withholding sex. The bottom line is that in a power struggle, both lose.

If you suspect you are in a power struggle with your spouse, keep asking yourself, "Why do I have to win? Why do I have to come out on top to feel good about me?" Try to realize that your self-worth does not depend on controlling your spouse. Of course, the trick is to recognize the power struggle when you are in it. A good clue is when one spouse resists a perfectly reasonable request from the other. It's not the request but what is perceived as domination that is resisted. Stop, identify the power struggle, pull back, start over!

The most difficult problem with power struggles is the complication of stereotypical masculine and feminine roles. Many men equate manhood with being in control. They think that if they are not ruling the marriage with iron fists they are somehow weak, objects of ridicule, "henpecked" husbands. In many marriages power comes from money. The one with the biggest income calls the shots. In most marriages the man is that person. Wives often buy into these roles for years before they grow up, becoming progressively unhappier. For subservient spouses are neither to be desired, nor admired. There is no growth, no real intimacy in an unequal relationship. The controlled partner plays games, hides true emotions behind a mask, withdraws from the marriage and maybe the world. This is fake love and an unhealthy relationship.

The good news is that marriages are moving toward partnerships rather than the parent-child relationships of the 1950s and 60s. Husbands, if you suspect that your idea of the masculine role is causing your marriage problems, try the following experiment. Come home from work and help your wife do what has to be done until the two of you finish. Do not sit down to read the paper until she can sit down to read the paper too! You will notice incredible results, results certainly worth giving up your role for. Remember, when you divide responsibilities, you double your time together!

Rejection

An underlying issue in many arguments is actually the perception of rejection or lack of caring. If Jane is angry because Tony stays away from home so much, the anger is probably from feeling personally rejected. If Richard is angry because Kathy is flirting with other men, he is probably feeling she doesn't care for him any more. If Susan is upset because Joe watches so much TV, she is probably taking it as a rejection of her company. If Ken is angry because Hazel spends so much energy on the children, he probably believes she loves them more than him. If you are upset because of some behavior of your spouse, ask yourself if that behavior says to you, "That must mean I am not loved or cared for. That must mean he doesn't want me or want to be with me." If the answer is yes, communicate that concern to your spouse and forget the superficial issue.

Prestige

In many fights the issue isn't as important as "proving I am right." If I am wrong, then my prestige or status is affected, so I go through marriage insisting that my way is the right way, my thoughts the right thoughts. The subtitle for "Why are you so quiet (talkative, disorganized, messy, etc.)" is "Why aren't you more like me?" There is, however, rarely a "right" or "wrong" way. It's usually a matter of perception. You automatically process everything in terms of your own beliefs, values, goals, and experience. Therefore, everything is "right"—for you! Married couples are like two people on opposite sides of a fence with one side painted white and one side painted brown. One will insist the fence is white and one will insist it is brown! They are both right! Recognize that you and your spouse are like two painters painting a picture of the same landscape. They will see and paint the landscape differently, yet both will be "right." Accept that you are both right and get on with solving your problem!

Space

Couples often enter marriage with very different needs for intimacy and/or personal "space." When they do, trouble crops up—and quickly! The one needing freedom or "space" pulls away more and more as the one needing closeness pursues more and more. This may be related to independence and dependence. The independent person likes freedom; the dependent one needs attachment. It's easy to see how arguments over anything involving interests, activities, time, or communication can have the hidden messages, "Give me space" or "Come closer."

It's an extremely rare marriage in which both want or need total togetherness. Most of us need some breathing room, air, space, separate interests, and separate friends. Marriage does not mean being joined at the hip. A healthy marriage is made up of two independent, self-reliant people with separate as well as mutual interests. A chain doesn't work in a marriage, and it really doesn't make any difference whether the chain is made of steel or gold!

If you believe that space is a real issue in your marriage, remember this rule: Never pursue a withdrawer. The more you go after a withdrawer, the more he/she will withdraw. Learn to be your own person. Plan separate time for yourself; engage in more activities with friends. As you back up, your spouse will move closer to you. Many people need to learn closeness. For some, closeness is like being devoured.

Generally it's the wife who keeps pushing for more closeness. She defines herself more by relationships; they are her identity. If this is true for you, learn to see yourself as a whole person apart from your husband. Find a boundary between yourself and your husband. Don't give up everything for him; have separate interests. Continue to see old friends and make new separate ones.

The key to pinpointing the real issues behind your fights is awareness. If you suspect that you are not arguing about the real issues, you can do one of two things. In the heat of an argument try to come up with what your needs are at the time that are not being met. Then complete this sentence, "I need . . ." and let your spouse respond to that. Or you can look at your spouse and carefully ask, "What do you want from me right now?" Then be prepared to address that issue. Otherwise you might end up constantly arguing without ever addressing your real problems.

CHAPTER 8

The Marriage Contract

Now that you have negotiated some of the conflicts in your marriage, think about putting the results in the form of a contract. A marital contract, like any other contract, is a written agreement for behavior change by both partners. It structures behavioral exchanges between spouses in terms of Who does What to Whom and When. The behaviors and their consequences must be clearly spelled out, and they must be understandable and acceptable to both partners.

Some people believe that contracts have no place in a marriage—that they're much too formal and impersonal. A marriage contract is a cold and hard way, they say, to deal with something as warm and alive as a marriage. However, contracting can be one of the most important skills a couple can learn. Some of the advantages are:

1. It keeps you goal-oriented, because you both

know an end product that will be written down is
what you are working toward.

2. Because contracts deal with specific behavior,
not generalities, they force you to deal with specifics.
You must each specify, perhaps for the first time,
exactly what you want from the other and exactly
what you are willing to give.

3. Humans generally want predictability in their
relationships. A contract supplies the control that
leads to predictability.

4. The very acts of agreeing to something and
signing the agreement generate a higher level of
commitment. It is less likely that you will forget
something to which your signature has been affixed.

5. Contracts that contain built-in rewards can
make good use of the powerful force of operant conditioning. Simply stated, behavior that is rewarded
or reinforced is more likely to occur again! The rewards become incentives for increasing the frequency of positive behaviors.

6. All marriages operate under contracts anyway,
if you think of a marriage as your concept of your
obligations to and benefits from the marital relationship. Since everyone has these expectations, it is
much better for them to be conscious and explicit,
rather than conscious but not verbalized, or even
beyond awareness.

7. Contracts are an easy and visible means for
evaluating your progress as a couple.

If you have extremely negative reactions to marital contracts, they are not absolutely necessary. A
contract as an end product is not nearly as valuable
as the process of conflict negotiation that you

learned. However, we urge you to give it a try. You live in a contract culture anyway. You sign a contract when you charge something on a credit card, order materials through the mail, pledge money to a church, borrow money, enter school or employment, or seek professional services. Virtually every interaction that you have with others is governed by a formal or informal contract that clarifies your expectations and guarantees that your investments will be reciprocated. Why, then, not marriage, which surely ranks as our primary relationship. Remember, you do desire change, or you wouldn't have this book. Research shows that the contracting procedure alone has contributed to a significant level of change in marriages!

Assignment

The first step in making a contract is for each spouse to make positive, specific requests of the other that will begin to make the relationship more rewarding. These should be worded positively: "Pick up your clothes from the floor," as opposed to "Don't be so sloppy." Asking a spouse to *stop* doing something often causes a defense of that behavior. The requests must also be worded specifically. "Be more affectionate" is much too vague. "Kiss me good-bye when you leave" lets your spouse know exactly what you want. Come up with at least three things you would like your spouse to do. In the appendix is a list of sample requests. Your own requests need to be more specific than those on the list —designate time, place, frequency. You might use the behaviors that you have negotiated earlier.

Now exchange behaviors and select one of your spouse's requests to do, or two, or even all three. Your spouse will do the same. Agree to follow your spouse's request more frequently during the next week—but only for one week! Going longer than one week in the beginning will mean that you won't get the feedback you need. The requested behavior must be specific and observable to both of you. If you have difficulty negotiating exchanges, go back over the chapter on conflict negotiation and use the skills recommended there. Now fill out a contract form spelling out your agreement. You can choose between two types. The first is the "Tit-for-Tat" agreement, in which one or more of one spouse's behaviors are directly exchanged for one or more of the other spouse's behaviors.

COUPLE REQUEST INDEX

Doing a household repair
Giving me time alone
Going out to dinner
Spending a weekend with me away from home
Talking on phone to me
Going out to movie/bar, etc.
Playing sports with me
Watching TV with me
Washing the car
Mowing the lawn
Getting the car fixed
Doing some gardening
Giving me spending money

Initiating sex
Putting children to bed
Making some extra money
Telling me you love me
Spending time with the kids
Making me breakfast
Complimenting my appearance
Helping kids with homework
Starting a conversation with me
Asking about my feelings
Paying a bill
Helping dress the children
Listening to my problems
Laughing with me
Balancing the checkbook
Helping with dinner
Preparing an entire meal
Doing some shopping for things we need
Cleaning up house (or portion)
Running an errand
Setting the alarm clock
Doing the dishes
Doing the laundry
Feeding the pets
Meeting me for lunch
Mending my clothes
Taking out the garbage
Responding to my advances
Babysitting while I am out
Hugging or kissing me
Surprising me with a gift
Shopping with me
Having dinner ready on time

Wearing pleasing clothing
Helping discipline the kids
Coming to bed with me
Holding the door for me
Planning the budget
Asking for my opinion
Being nice to my friends
Playing cards with me

The other is a "Reward Contract," in which each request is not necessarily exchanged for the spouse's, but is rewarded if accomplished. Either type can be beneficial. The major difference is that in the Reward Contract you must fulfill your responsibility before you get your reward, and in the Tit-for-Tat contract you carry our your responsibility and assume your spouse will do the same. The Reward Contract allows each person to comply with the terms of the contract independently of the other, thus avoiding recriminations over who did what first. Try them both and see which works best for you.

Some guidelines for contracting are:

1. Negotiate without coercing.

2. Make the terms simple, specific, and clear.

3. Make sure the contract provides advantages to each spouse over the status quo.

4. Limit requests to one week in the beginning.

5. Give anything a try. Remember you are not setting anything in concrete. Everything is renegotiable.

6. Don't wait for your spouse to do his/her item.

Proceed in good faith, assuming that your spouse will do his/her part.

7. Rewards do not have to be something provided by your spouse. Some possibilities are a new dress, some free time, etc.

8. Place the contract on the refrigerator or mirror where it will be seen.

9. Don't quit your part of the bargain if you suspect your partner is not keeping his/hers. Instead, schedule another session to discuss it.

Your contract can be as creative as your imagination. A bonus may be added as an extra incentive for a partner's compliance with the contract for several weeks.

At the end of a week, meet with your spouse and evaluate how well you each fulfilled the contract. If you are both satisfied with the current terms of the contract and want to continue it, you can then make a permanent one. If you were dissatisfied, use the communication skills you have learned to refine, revise, or restructure the contract. If your contract was a total disaster, start all over with completely different issues that may be less emotionally charged or easier to comply with. Start now to use your contracting skills to resolve any conflict in your marriage. As you gain skill in asking for change up front and in positive ways, you will begin to notice many refreshing changes in your marriage!

WHAT TO NEGOTIATE,
WHAT TO IGNORE

Before we leave the subject of conflict negotiation, we must discuss one last critical subject: Exactly what do we choose to ask our spouse to negotiate? Absolutely everything that causes us the slightest bit of discomfort? Unfortunately, that is the way most married people operate. Most people want—and really expect—an unrealistic perfection in their spouses. It's not clear when these unrealistic expectations of marriage begin. A recent national survey disclosed that the main reasons for divorce are no longer desertion, finances, religious differences, brutality, or adultery, as they were a generation ago. Instead, the three leading complaints are problems with communication, problems with child rearing, and sexual dissatisfaction. Couples now have the idea that they should always be able to communicate well, raise children with no problems, and enjoy fulfilled sex lives!

Anyone who works in the social services, media, or publishing fields has to share the responsibility for this state of affairs. Behavioral scientists (psychologists, counselors, social workers) have tried to improve many aspects of married life, such as communication, sex, and child rearing but in doing so, they have raised our expectations until we perceive problems even when there aren't really problems. Before the media provided new definitions of what marriages were supposed to be, these "problems" rarely existed.

Instead of realizing that marriages are unbelievably difficult, and that there will always be a lot of stress and a lot of problems in the best of them, we assume that something like perfection is possible. We have been so bombarded with what a relationship should be like that we dwell on the ways that our marriages fall short. But all marriages have areas of great disagreement and great difficulty—some of which will never change—and there will always be something to worry us and to be upset about. If we try communication or conflict negotiation skills and they don't help significantly, our doubts snowball. We wonder what is wrong with our spouse, what is wrong with us, are we still in love, do we need more counseling?

The truth is that even the best relationships have hard times. And overblown expectations only make the bad times worse. We must accept—as difficult as it is—that bad feelings, bad fights, and unresolvable incompatibilities are integral and inescapable parts of marriage! And by "bad feelings," we don't mean irritation or disappointment; we mean cold-as-ice withdrawal or blinding rage. By "bad fights," we don't mean polite little arguments; we mean dish-throwing, obscenity-screaming, dirty fighting. By "incompatibilities," we don't mean she likes the beach and he likes the mountains; we mean differences so great a computer couldn't have come up with any two people more opposite. Again, these are almost inescapable. If you don't believe this, ask any of your married friends who will level with you.

What, then, do you do if you have been taught that trying a little bit harder will make things perfect, just like they are "supposed" to be, and you find out that it just doesn't work?

You may not like the answer, but it is the answer. Whether you call it acceptance, tolerance, ignoring, or overlooking, the idea is the same. Remember that we said that there is no clear relationship between compatibility of personality traits and marital satisfaction. What does predict a happy marriage is not how compatible you are, but how you handle your incompatibilities! The more you can accept, tolerate, and even respect your spouse's differentness the happier you will be.

Overlooking each other's "warts" is a vital element in marriage, one that is necessary if a marriage is to survive. Marriage is a lot like buying a record. You buy it for what's on one side, but the flip side comes with it. You have to take that, too! Tolerance and acceptance of each other's weak spots, likes, dislikes, and differentness are all important if you are sincerely committed to marriage. The only alternatives are divorce or a world of frustration and pain. There are some things you will never change in your spouse. And there is no other partner out there who will be "perfect" for you. We've already talked about the color of the grass on the other side of the fence!

Holding unrealistic expectations about marriage is what some counselors call the "Utopia Syndrome." Utopia, as you may remember from high school English, is a place that is perfect, but is "Nowhere." It doesn't exist. Seeking utopia in a marriage will doom you to a lifetime of unfulfillment and frustration. If you are striving for perfection in your marriage, you have taken your first steps toward divorce or despair.

To compound the problem the changes that come with life make acceptance and tolerance necessary. Acceptance and tolerance are actually a process—an ongoing process. Few of us wake up on our twenty-fifth anniversary and find we are the same people we were when we got married. Nor are we married to the same person! Again, the ability to adjust expectations and accept change, even while changing together, is the secret to a long-term successful marriage.

All right then—we agree: acceptance, tolerance, and overlooking is the answer. But what is the secret for achieving it? It's easy to say but hard to do. We would like to suggest that you think of your spouse as a gift from God, which he or she surely is. This gift from God can be appreciated as it is without thought of change, just like a gift from God in nature. If you are walking on the beach and see a spectacular sunset, you don't call out to God, "A little more purple over behind the waves, please!" Or, "Would you mind giving us a little less orange in the back?" Of course not! You enjoy the always different sunsets exactly as they are. Do the same with your spouse. People are just as much gifts from God as sunsets!

The famous psychologist, Albert Ellis, has another way of saying the same thing. He says that all disturbed marital interaction arises when each spouse reacts badly to the normal frustrations of marriage and the abnormal demands of others, thus accentuating those frustrations and demands. Most individuals respond anxiously or angrily to even a relatively good life situation, since they have basically irrational or illogical attitudes or philosophies. They respond particularly badly to marriage, because it is, at best, exceptionally difficult, and our expectations are exceptionally unrealistic. Ellis vigorously challenges his marriage counseling clients to challenge their assumptions about what their spouse's behavior should be. When his clients work at changing their neurosis-creating assumptions, significant personality changes follow and their marriages almost always improve.

If you and your partner have conscientiously applied the principles of conflict negotiation that we have described, and in spite of all efforts still have unresolved problems, ask yourselves the following questions:

1. Is this worth fighting over? Is it a legitimate bone to pick?

2. Are you just in a rotten mood or overreacting to a trivial situation?

3. Is this a reasonable request to make, or something that will probably never change?

4. Are you demanding that your spouse be perfect, live his/her life according to your expectations, and never frustrate you?

Your answers to these questions will indicate if you need to practice the gentle art of acceptance. As a matter of fact, ask yourselves these questions whenever you have a problem with your spouse. Your answers may determine whether you should verbalize your problem or learn the art of editing. It may well be a time to keep your mouth shut. Open communication does not mean "letting it all hang-out." Total, uncensored communication usually has negative results. In almost every unhappy marriage there is a spouse who says things best left unsaid.

Make a list now of all the minor irritants of your spouse. Write down everything you can't stand. Now burn the list in the fireplace. Do this once a month. You'll find this symbolic burning has real power!

CHAPTER 9

Nurturing the Love Relationship

This chapter deals with an issue that we are all concerned with at one time or another—our emotional feelings toward our spouse. This may be your major concern right now. You may not feel that you are in love with your spouse anymore, or he/she with you. You may be wondering if it is possible to recapture the warm, loving feelings you once had. Or you may be wondering what you can do to keep love alive. We hope you have already begun to think about how your marriage got into trouble, and what you can do to prevent it happening again.

There are two important points here. First, a marriage is a living, breathing entity that must be nurtured in order to stay alive. There is no such thing as "getting married and living happily ever after." Those are the most misleading words that pen ever put to paper. If you get married and expect to stay happily in love without doing anything for your marriage, you'll wind up with a dead marriage. A marriage is like a plant. If you buy a plant and put it on the shelf, doing absolutely nothing for or to it, it will surely die—some faster than others, but die they all will. But if you water it, fertilize it, give it air and light, pull out the weeds, pick off the bugs, in other words, nurture it, it will grow and delight you. Your marriage is the same. Put it on the shelf and it will die. Water it, fertilize it, get rid of the bugs and weeds, just nurture it, and it will grow and delight you. It is either one or the other: growth or death. A marriage like the moon, is either waxing or waning. Accordingly, your marriage either increases or decreases in strength. This chapter gives you the skills and concepts needed to continue to nurture your marriage so that it will continue to grow and delight you.

Another point is that loving feelings grow because you do these things. Couples do not "fall out of love." Instead, they simply stop working on their relationship. Once you start working on your relationship again, you can fall in love again. Remember, behavioral changes precede changes in feelings. If you begin to act loving, the loving feelings will return. The important question is not "Am I in love with my spouse?" Couples who were once in love can almost always reignite their love. The key question is "Was I ever in love with my spouse?" If your answer is "yes," this chapter will move you well on your way to getting there again.

WHAT IS LOVE?

It is impossible to discuss ways to recapture love or ensure the growth of love without first speaking about the nature of love. Exactly what is love? Although great writers throughout history have failed to agree on a definition of this elusive emotion, we find it necessary to add to the discussion. This is because so many married people have truly unrealistic expectations, not only of marriage, but of what actually constitutes love.

Perhaps it is easier to say what love is not. Love is not infatuation or passion. It is not what makes the heart beat faster. Infatuation is a wild, ecstatic feeling of having "fallen in love." Although the feeling may be wonderful, it is not based on reality. The object of an infatuation is idealized and overvalued. Faults are denied or literally not seen. Thus the saying, "Love is blind." Infatuation is never permanent! Because the feelings are so intense, they can't be sustained.

Love is also not lust. Lust is pure sexual desire, and this is obviously self-directed. Lust can function separately without infatuation or love. But when lust is mixed with infatuation or love, as it often is, there is a synergistic effect. This means one effect enhances the others, making it difficult to distinguish one from the other.

Because love usually starts with infatuation and lust, many marriages fall apart because people confuse the inevitable settling-in process—the shift from infatuation—with a lessening of love. Love is not a feeling. Feelings are never constant. They come and go. If you overemphasize the feeling of infatuation, when you "fall out of love" you may think that your marriage is over!

But that doesn't mean you just settle for "companionship." True love offers much more. You can keep the spark of intense love alive. The first step is differentiating the spark from the flames. When you first light the charcoal in a grill, there's a great burst of flame. That's the infatuation. But you can't cook on it. It's not until the flames are gone and you have a bed of white-hot coals that you can do any cooking. Love is the bed of white-hot coals.

True love is more an active process than an emotion. You do not "fall into" true love. Both you and your spouse create it, because it has to be reciprocal. Neither infatuation nor lust has to be reciprocal. Love is characterized by a deep commitment not only to each other, but to the relationship itself. It is based on mutual purposes and shared goals. It is this emotional commitment that must be absolute, rather than the emotion itself. Love is a decision!

Love should not be thought of as a permanent concrete solid that is either visibly there or not. It's more like a gas, coming and going in varying strengths, maybe visible, maybe not. During the course of a long marriage couples will experience many cycles—good times, bad times, times of closeness, times of distance. Unless you realize that this is normal, you may mistake a time of distance as the end of love.

Maybe one advantage of marriage is that when you fall out of love, it keeps you together until you perhaps fall in again!

At least those of us whose marriages have lasted many years know that time is on our side.

RECIPROCITY REVIEWED

Let's begin our discussion of how to nurture the love relationship with a review of the principle of reciprocity: you get what you give and you give what you get. Marital happiness is the result of each spouse having needs met through positive behaviors and then reciprocating through positive behaviors. When you do loving things for your partner, he/she experiences the relationship as rewarding and is more likely to do and say the loving things that please you. And so it goes. You got into the habit of trying to please your partner and reinforcing him/her when he/she pleases you when you practiced the exercise, Catch Your Partner Pleasing You. Now we are going to focus on specifically loving or affectionate things and make them an integral part of your marriage.

Please don't underestimate the power of affection, even if your partner professes not to care that much about it! You can see for yourself the difference it makes. Especially if your partner has ever strayed, make affection a part of your life. Most people who have affairs are looking not for sex, but are starved for affection. They say things like "My spouse never held my hand, never kissed me or touched me unless we were having sex, never told me I looked nice, never gave me a compliment, never said I love you." These people were starving to death, emotionally. If there's never any food on your table, you will eventually eat off someone else's table!

What follows is a list of Loving Things to Do that can get you started thinking of affectionate things you can do for your spouse. This list is only to get you started. You will be the best judge of what makes your partner happy, so add as many as you can.

List of Loving Things to Do

1. Bring home flowers.
2. Say "I love you" more often.
3. Cook a favorite meal.
4. Send a card.
5. Touch more often.
6. Take him/her out for a meal.
7. Spend more time talking (actually set aside a period of time).
8. Bring home a plant.
9. Take him/her out for a night on the town.
10. Write a special poem.
11. Schedule a baby sitter and plan a meal or time alone for the two of you.
12. Plan a "game time" where the two of you play something together.
13. Scratch his/her back (or a nice massage lasting over five minutes).
14. Put love notes in his/her lunch bag, under the pillow, under the dinner plate . . .
15. Buy a special gift.
16. Serve breakfast in bed.

17. Find out his/her sexual preferences and add spice to your lovemaking.

18. Give a compliment.

19. Give a reassuring hug each day.

20. Give a kiss each morning and evening.

21. Make a note to remember special days and do something nice.

22. Help in the kitchen (cooking or with dishes).

23. Appear interested by encouraging him/her to talk about how he/she feels or how the day went.

24. Take a walk together after dinner (this would be a good time to talk about feelings, how to solve problems, etc.).

25. Hold his/her hand (when walking, shopping, etc.).

26. Ask your partner what he/she would like, what needs he/she has, what would make him/her happy.

Remember to add to this list. There are thousands of possibilities.

Do at least two loving things for or to your spouse every day from now on. If this seems formidable, maybe you are thinking loving things are always big things. Rather, it's the little things that count. A recent study concluded that in the average marriage there are two hundred and fifty opportunities per day to show your partner you care. These can be as insignificant as kissing his/her eyelids awake in the morning. Don't let lack of money be an excuse for not doing loving things. That's a copout! Affection doesn't cost anything. Most people would rather have a wildflower picked on the way home and presented with love than a dozen red roses presented by the florist!

After you are in the habit of doing loving things for your spouse daily, start instituting a "Love Day" once a week. On Love Days you double or triple the number of loving things you have been doing. Don't announce your Love Day. If you think your partner has given you a Love Day, ask if this is true. If your partner doesn't acknowledge a Love Day, ask if it was noticed. This reinforces the importance of noticing and commenting on loving actions.

You may think that doing loving and affectionate things for your spouse is "forced" or "mechanical," because you don't feel loving or affectionate. That's OK! That forced, mechanical feeling will soon be replaced by spontaneous, warm feelings if you continue to do these things.

Down Memory Lane

Pick a time each week—a few minutes is all that is necessary—to walk down memory lane with your spouse. During this time you will share one memory of your marriage that had special meaning for one or both of you. Memories can be verbal or material. A "memory" is defined as any event, place, ritual, souvenir, or object that carries special meaning for you. Your walk down memory lane will be an actual show-and-tell, where you display or describe your memory and your feelings about it. You can sing your special song, describe a memory of your honeymoon, anniversary, holiday, or vacation, or any other memory associated with love and joy. Or you can produce any object such as a photograph, an old shoe that was tied to the bumper of your wedding car, old clothes worn on a special occasion, or a souvenir bought on a vacation together. If you have to rummage through the attic or garage, so much the better.

Special times in the past can be memories, also. Laura Ann and Tom used to go to the "Rock Pile," an old service station made of rocks where the college kids hung out, on Friday afternoons when they attended the University of North Carolina at Chapel Hill. They drank beer, sang Carolina songs, and laughed with their friends. The term "rock pile," Friday afternoon beer parties, and Carolina songs all have special meaning for them now. Even negative memories can be remembered with warmth and humor. Laura Ann beat Tom in miniature golf on their honeymoon, leading to their first argument, and many a laugh since. Now any game of miniature golf or friendly competition where Laura Ann might win brings warm memories of a wonderful honeymoon.

Rituals also belong to the memory category. Christy and Lee used to have breakfast in bed on Sunday mornings during those carefree days before children. Now that the children are much older the ritual has been reinstated, appreciated and enjoyed all the more because of the memories!

So make your appointment to go down Memory Lane once each week, and continue to do this for the duration of your marriage. After all, you are constantly accumulating memories and will be as long as you are married. Something you do or have today will be your memory for tomorrow. Walking down

Memory Lane is one of the most rewarding things you can do. Your walks down Memory Lane will bring back warm, positive memories of mutual love, romance, shared joy, and affection. They are invaluable for helping couples get back in touch with the positive feeling that may be buried deeply under layers of hostility and pain.

THE OXYGEN OF INTIMACY

If one word can describe the kinds of warm, close feelings we have been discussing, it is probably the word "intimacy." Intimacy is a state of mutual trust and acceptance between two individuals that permits open communication, emotional sharing, and a willingness to be deeply known by another person. Simply stated, intimacy involves closeness, openness, and vulnerability. Many think only of the sexual relationship when using the word, but intimacy in a marriage goes far beyond the sexual aspect. It is the bedrock of any successful marriage. Intimacy can grow deeper or it can disappear. If it disappears, the quality vital for a full and satisfying marriage fades away. The marriage may survive, but there will be loneliness. Intimacy doesn't just magically appear or disappear. You must make a conscious decision to commit yourself to intimacy! "Love at first sight" may or may not exist, but there is no such thing as "instant intimacy." True intimacy needs time to take root and grow.

There are three things that will keep intimacy alive in your marriage or restore it if it has been lost (or was never there!). We call these three items the "oxygen of intimacy." Though these things can't guarantee that intimacy will grow, it is certain that intimacy will not exist without them. They are the "Three T's": Time, Talk, and Touch.

Time

On a physical level, sheer time spent in each other's company relating to each other is necessary for intimacy to grow. There is no way around it. We're talking about "quality time," in which your attention is focused on each other or on experiencing things together. Quality time implies that there is no time crunch, no crowds, and no sense of doing five things at once. We have never known a marriage to get in trouble in which both partners continued to take time to talk, do things together, share worries and dreams, or just enjoy the simple things with each other that they originally did. But couples stop taking this time together for several reasons. The first is pure apathy. Not realizing the importance of time together, they simply drift into separate interests and separate worlds. Because they don't consciously make time to do anything together they become "two ships passing in the night." They are "married singles," playing double solitaire.

Another reason is a work-ethic mindset. We live in an action-oriented culture. The idea of just spending time with a spouse—maybe just sitting, or talking, or reading, or looking at a sunset—can be perceived as wasted time. How sad! This attitude is difficult to change because it involves changing a philosophy of life.

A third reason is that couples often see the situation as unavoidable. Because of jobs and other responsibilities, they say it is just impossible to spend any more time together. Regrettable, but still impossible. Again, how sad! The truth is however that we all make time for what is important to us. We do not find the time, we make it! There may be no easy answers to this dilemma. Sometimes you have to give up a much loved activity, or a job, or make a major change in your lifestyle. It can mean less money and other sacrifices. But if marriage is truly your number-one priority, these are sacrifices that have to be made. If you see time as your problem, remember one thing: nobody on his/her death bed ever said, "I wish I'd spent more time at the office or with my business."

The following suggestions will help you get started on getting time with your spouse back into your marriage:

1. The biggest obstacle to a couple's time together is not from their work, but from what they see as "social obligations." Make a list of everything the two of you do besides your work. Prioritize them, then be ruthless about slashing the bottom ones off the list. PTA, the school board, Lion's Club, Cancer Society, or charity work, are all worthwhile activities, but something's got to give!

2. Follow the example of new lovers. They go to great lengths to make every moment count. Watches must be synchronized to ensure time together. Their time is well orchestrated, and they rarely keep each

other waiting. Other appointments are missed and many a red light has been run to keep an appointment with a lover. You must make the same effort to get time with your spouse. When you arrange time together, whether it's a luncheon date or a weekend out of town, refuse to allow anything to take precedence over that time! Pretend you are mad, passionate lovers who may never see each other again.

3. Take an occasional weekend trip away from home without the kids. Even if you just stay at a motel in town, the excitement of getting away can bring romance back into your marriage. If you think this is a luxury you can't afford, use your creativity to think up solutions. Trade off babysitting with a neighbor or relative, and just go camping in the woods!

4. You may be having difficulty thinking of things you might do with your spouse that you would enjoy. Couples usually get stuck in routine ways of living together. But there is no limit to the experiences you can have together once you give yourself permission to leave the safety of your routine. On the next page we list some activities that couples have said are enjoyable or fun for them. See if you can find some experiences on this list you might like to try. They may be things you've never thought of or things you used to but no longer do. Talk to each other about which ones you'd be willing to try, then do them! Again, don't let lack of money be your excuse. How much does an evening walk cost? Or breakfast in bed? Or even a cup of coffee at a fast-food restaurant?

Perhaps it's impossible to find things you'd both

enjoy. Then trade off! She can go fishing with him this weekend; he can go to the concert with her next weekend. The point remains—decide together on things you'll do, then do them!

TOGETHERNESS ACTIVITIES

Going bowling
Taking dancing lessons
Riding bicycles
Camping
Going to a museum
Going sailing
Playing miniature golf
Going swimming in the nude
Reading out loud to each other
Eating breakfast out
Bar hopping
Playing in the snow
Backpacking
Going dancing
Taking pictures
Going to a movie
Playing badminton
Playing tennis
Playing cards
Gardening
Taking a bath or shower together
Going skiing
Going to a concert

Taking a drive in the country
Getting up to see the sunrise
Cooking something unusual
Taking a walk in the woods
Going to an auction
Visiting friends
Going on a picnic
Listening to music
Meeting for lunch or coffee
Fishing
Working with crafts
Playing frisbee
Going to a circus
Going canoeing
Jogging/going for a walk
Playing charades
Looking at the stars
Joining a new club
Going horseback riding

Dining alone by candlelight
Flying a kite
Going to a movie
Exploring new places
Going to the park
Going shopping
Playing pool
Going to a ball game
Going skating
Going to the races
Doing exercises
Looking at home movies
Making home improvements
Painting
Going to church
Eating at new restaurant
Making love

Talk

Back to communication. No matter how much time you spend together, you will never really get to know or relate to your spouse unless you learn to talk to each other. In every truly happy marriage the partners spend time just talking to each other! Because talking together in a relaxed way is usually the first thing to go when a marriage gets into trouble, we suggest the following ways to get it back in your marriage:

1. Couples must touch base often, daily if possible, in order to know "what's going on" with each other. We recommend a "Touch Base Time" of at least twenty minutes every evening to accomplish this. Touch Base Time should consist of two different kinds of talking, each of them critical. One kind without the other leaves a void.

The first kind of talking is gossipy conversation. This is simply sharing the day's events with each other in a relaxed way: who you saw, what you did, who called, possible future plans, etc. etc. Spend at least half of Touch Base time on this.

The other half of the time is spent free associating what is going on within you right now. Your spouse might know a lot about what you are doing, but not much at all about what you are thinking and feeling. You may share feelings, hopes, fears, joy, and sorrow, but not facts. You may share goals, dreams, plans, fantasies. Children who are best friends do this. If you'd like your spouse to be your best friend, try to do the same.

2. If sharing feelings is difficult for you, begin slowly and use crutches. One crutch is dream analysis. Many couples discuss last night's dreams in the morning and try to figure out the dreams together. Sentence stems are also crutches. If you have trouble beginning to share, take turns completing the following sentences to each other.

—One thing I'd like you to know about me is . . .

—One thing I wish you understood about me is . . .

—One thing I wish I understood about you is . . .

—Sometimes I feel great when you . . .

—Sometimes I feel terrible when you . . .

—As I sit here listening to you . . .

—If the way I'm feeling was a song it would be . . .

—If you could hear what I cannot say . . .

—One thing I am aware of about you is . . .

—One thing I imagine about you is . . .

—One thing I know about you that you aren't aware of is . . .

—One thing I love about our relationship is . . .

3. Fantasy questions are excellent. Take turns asking each other some of the following questions, then make up your own. The list is endless.

—If you had a million dollars how would you spend it?

—If you could be anyone in the world, who would it be?

—If you could live anywhere in the world for one year, where would it be?

—If you could make love to anyone in the world, who would it be?

—If you could live during any period in history, when would it be?

—If you had one year to live what would you do?

—If you could do anything in the world and get paid for it, what would it be?

—If you could have three wishes granted, what would they be?

4. Consider making Touch Base Time a walk together after dinner. Did you ever notice it's almost impossible to do anything else while walking except talk? There will be no TV to watch, nothing to distract you, no phone to answer or bell to ring. Also the benefits to your health will be great!

Touch

Probably the most powerful form of communication in a marriage is physical, nonsexual touching. Touch can express a warmth that words cannot possibly convey. Studies show that babies who aren't touched often get sick and even die. And the need for touch stays with us for life. "Skin hunger" is a fact recognized by mental health experts for years. There is an important connection between touching and a person's sense of security and self-esteem. Even experiments with monkeys and chimpanzees demonstrate that they become neurotic, irritable, and unable to relate when deprived of touch.

Especially if you have trouble expressing your love verbally for your spouse, it's important to say it with your hands. Touching is a reassurance that "you are loved"—a reassurance that we all need. Yet often any touching other than sexual disappears from marriage. We are not talking here about touching that leads to sex, but rather the little hugs and squeezes, the tender kiss, the arm around the shoulder, holding hands, a massage, snuggling, sitting close together, and gentle touches in passing.

A common pattern that leads to the disappearance of touch is when he doesn't touch except sexually, and she doesn't touch because it is interpreted by him as a sexual signal. Yet most women crave physical affection apart from sex. Women learn not to touch when every touch leads to bed. Ironically, one of the best ways for a man to improve his sex life is to begin to consistently touch his spouse lovingly and nonsexually! Try it and see!

Many people are uncomfortable with touch. Perhaps they have grown up in a nondemonstrative family. Perhaps they regard touch as an invasion of personal space or privacy. Still touch is part of the oxygen of intimacy. Learning to touch again, or maybe for the first time, may be somewhat uncomfortable at first. But if you consistently make it a part of your marriage, you will not only become comfortable with it but will learn to like it. To help you get started, start doing the following things:

1. Lovingly hold your spouse (an unhurried, tender hug) at least twice a day—perhaps when you part in the morning and when you come together at night.

2. Estimate or chart how often you and your spouse engage in nonsexual touching each week. Increase that by 50 percent next week, 100 percent the week after and 200 percent the week after that, and 400 percent the week after that! Simply do it and do it now!

A final word of warning. We mentioned before that all couples will experience cycles of times of closeness, times of distance. Probably all of us need more breathing room or separateness some times more than other times. Obviously, therefore, the intensity of the intimacy of your marriage will vary from time to time. Your goal is to have an ongoing intimate relationship, not one that is intimate and intense at all times. To expect otherwise is to set yourself up for disappointment.

CHAPTER 10

The Sexual Relationship

It's no secret that a troubled marriage usually shows itself in the bedroom. One study found that 80 percent of couples seeking marriage counseling were sexually dissatisfied. Although some unhappy marriages maintain an excellent sexual relationship, and sexual problems are sometimes present in otherwise happy marriages, for the most part the health of the marriage is reflected in the health of the sexual relationship.

Considering this, you may wonder why we left discussion of the sexual relationship to last. The truth is that the sexual relationship can rarely be dealt with before the total relationship improves. Sex is a logical expression of intimate marriages, and the quality of the social relationship must improve before the sexual relationship can. If open communication and a caring atmosphere are not in place, it won't do much good to try to improve your sex life.

Though dissatisfaction with the sexual relationship is common among troubled marriages, it is a myth that unsatisfactory sex life is a major cause of bad marriages. Sexual problems are a symptom of marital discord, not a cause. Now that you have hopefully greatly improved the level of communication and caring behaviors in your marriage, you have hopefully eliminated the main causes of your marital discord. Perhaps resolving the other issues in your marriage has automatically resolved the sexual ones. If not, we'll now move on to trying to improve your sexual relationship.

A word of caution: there may be severe problems that you will not be able to solve on your own. And such problems are made worse because improving the sexual functioning of your marriage, for reasons you'll soon see, is easy to sabotage. Also some sexual problems may have a physical basis and require a medical examination, like impotence and painful intercourse. In such cases outside help is indicated. (See chapter 11 "When More Help is Needed".) Please seek help, therefore, if you can't improve your sexual relationship on your own. Because the human sexual response is conditioned, it often responds well to "reconditioning." Sexual problems are like the rest of your marital problems—they usually have a solution.

Solving your sexual problems is a three-stage process. Take these stages in order. You will severely handicap yourselves if you try to get ahead of yourself.

STEP 1—INCREASING YOUR KNOWLEDGE ABOUT SEX

Many sexual problems arise from just one problem—ignorance about human sexuality. This comes about quite naturally. Because men and women differ significantly sexually, yet a marriage is made up of a man and a women, there are automatically different needs, wants, and expectations. The differences often remain hidden because of difficulties in discussing sex. We won't attempt to include in this book all the sexual information you might want or need. There are many excellent scholarly books available at your local bookstore or library that do that. The following list includes information on some of the most often misunderstood areas. If you read anything below that is a surprise to you, we strongly urge you to do some additional reading!

1. Quantity is usually more important for a man and quality is more important for a woman. If a husband gives his wife the kind of sexual experience she likes, the quantity of it might be less of a problem.

2. Many problems come from defining "sex" as intercourse. Intercourse is not the only way to have sex, it's one way. Many prefer other ways and can have orgasms only in other ways. Defining sex as intercourse can lead to concern with performance, which can lead to impotency and difficulty with orgasm.

3. Approximately 80 percent of women never have orgasms during intercourse without additional clitoral stimulation. A man not willing to satisfy his

wife manually or orally will likely have a frustrated wife.

4. Women, however, are not always as concerned with orgasm as men. Some women don't desire orgasm every time, and feel pressured by their spouses to have one.

5. For a woman an orgasm can be both a satisfaction and a stimulation. She can get aroused again very quickly after an orgasm and can have multiple orgasms. For a man an orgasm is a satisfaction only. It takes a while for him to become aroused again.

6. Afterplay is usually as important to a woman as foreplay. For most men, sex is over after orgasm.

7. Men are much more genitally oriented than women. Lovemaking for a woman means hugging and cuddling, plus kissing, caressing, and stroking all parts of the body.

8. Sex and emotions are closely joined for women. Just as most women simply aren't interested in sex without love, most women don't want sex if they are angry or upset.

9. For many women, foreplay begins at breakfast! That means they want to be treated nicely and lovingly before it's time for sex. Seduction is not the same thing as arousal. Seduction needs to begin hours before arousal!

10. The fear of unwanted pregnancy keeps many women from enjoying sex. The "pill" is the most effective form of contraception, but also the most dangerous. If your family is complete, a vasectomy may be the answer in your marriage.

11. Men have far more sexual fears than women

realize. Often their performance fears and fears of rejection make them seem uninterested in sex.

12. Men enjoy getting out of the aggressor role in sex from time to time. They like women to take an active role both in initiating sex and in bed.

STEP 2—INCREASING YOUR COMMUNICATION ABOUT SEX

A lack of communication about sex between partners has been clearly shown to be crucial in the development of sexual problems for most couples. It's easy to understand why. This is one area where our culture denies us the freedom to communicate openly. Women, especially, find it extremely difficult to talk about sex. There is no other area in our lives that is so contaminated by deeply held beliefs about ourselves, our bodies, what is right, what is wrong, what is shameful, what is private, what is sacred, what is dirty, what is exciting! (As you can see, your "sexual script" is a large part of your "marital script.") No wonder it is so difficult for couples to discuss sex. Neither partner can communicate what he/she would like, what feels good, and what doesn't.

In a marriage counselor's office, most sexual complaints are about frequency. That's the surface complaint, but often a cover. A lot of times when people say they don't want sex, what they really mean is they want it, but differently. Before you proceed, discuss the following questions with your spouse until you begin to feel comfortable communicating about sex. This may often be difficult, but after a while you'll find you are more at ease discussing sex. You may discover that your sexual problems will simply take care of themselves as they are discussed.

1. Am I happy with the frequency of sex? What would I prefer?

2. Am I happy with who initiates sex? What would I prefer?

3. What would be the greatest sexual experience I could imagine?

4. Am I happy with the time of day we have sex? What would I prefer?

5. Would I prefer my partner to be more aggressive? Less? How?

6. What length of time would I like to be spent in foreplay?

7. What activities would I like in foreplay?

8. What length of time would I like to be spent in intercourse?

9. Am I happy with the frequency of my orgasms? My partner's?

10. Am I satisfied with our birth control method? What would I prefer?

11. Where do I like to be touched? Caressed?

12. Where do I not like to be touched? Caressed?

13. Where do I like to be kissed?

14. Where do I not like to be kissed?

15. What sexual activities would I like to try?

16. What sexual activities really turn me off?

17. What is the one thing I have the most difficulty discussing about our sex life?

After you have thoroughly discussed these questions with your spouse, proceed with the third step.

STEP 3—ENHANCEMENT OF SENSUALITY

There is usually one major thing that prevents persons from enjoying the sensuality of a sexual experience. They become so aware of their own or their partner's responses that they become separate or split from their feelings. They become spectators observing the action. This is called "spectatoring" and it almost guarantees a loss of sensation, making erection or orgasm impossible. Worrying about performing instead of being immersed in the sensation makes performance difficult. Men are especially vulnerable to fears of sexual performance because of our culture's emphasis on erections as a symbol of manhood. Even one failure can bring fear of loss of virility—and each sexual experience becomes a test. Men can thus easily condition themselves to be spectators.

Sensuality is enhanced if there are no demands for performance. Therefore, sensual enhancement programs always initially forbid sexual intercourse. This is often a big relief; it allows the couple to relax and enjoy the sensuality of the sexual experience. But couples can sabotage themselves. If they become so aroused that they engage in intercourse, they have sacrificed long-term elimination of the spectator role for immediate pleasure.

One sensual enhancement technique is called "sensate focus." It is often used to help the three major sexual problems: impotence, premature ejaculation, and orgasmic dysfunction. Though this one technique will not eliminate all sexual problems, it goes a long way toward helping you enjoy your sexual relationship. Sensate focus, introduced by Masters and Johnson, is undoubtedly the single-most significant technique developed in sex therapy. It is called "sensate focus" because it focuses on sensation.

The goal of sensate focus is sensual pleasure, not sexual arousal. The only directive is to tune into the senses without pressure to perform. This frees couples to experience what occurs rather than concerning themselves with what the experience "should" be. Try this exercise only if you both feel comfortable enough to do so.

Sensate Focus

STEP 1

1. Agree to abstain from sexual intercourse throughout the sensate focus procedure. There must be no genital touching during Step 1.

2. Set aside anywhere from forty to ninety minutes in a warm, pleasant room that is secure from interruption. The lights should be on but not bright.

3. Take showers and then go to bed without any clothes on. Alternate being the Giver and Receiver. Use a lotion, such as baby oil. The Receiver lies on his/her stomach. The Giver gently caresses his/her entire body except for the genitals and breasts. Start with the back of the head, then ears, neck, back, sides, buttocks, thighs, legs, calves, feet. Take your time. Be gentle and creative. The Receiver just concentrates on his/her feelings. Do not worry about whether your spouse is getting tired or bored.

4. The Receiver must give the Giver feedback.

If something feels unpleasant, or if it is being done too fast, too hard or too lightly, say so. If something feels particularly good, say so.

5. Exchange roles. All the same instructions apply.

6. Reverse roles again and turn over. Now do the front the same way. Start with the head, face, and neck. Caress chest, belly, sides, thighs, legs, feet. Again, skip the genitals and breasts.

7. Exchange roles again.

8. Do Step 1 two or three times a week for one to two weeks before going to Step 2.

STEP 2

9. All of the rules of Step 1 apply except that the genitals and breasts are now included. As much time should be spent on the rest of the body as before, however. The goal is still pleasure, not orgasm. Caressing should be light and teasing, not the rhythmic, focused stimulation that leads to orgasm. Again, Receiver should not become distracted. Stay with the feelings and enjoy them. The Receiver may need to guide the hand of the Giver. Orgasm should be avoided, or postponed as long as possible. The Receiver may guide the Giver to a mode of stimulation that ends in orgasm, but it must be on the Receiver's initiation. Otherwise, you're back to where you started.

10. Step 2 should be done two or three times a week for one or two weeks.

11. After at least three weeks of sensate focus, the couple may incorporate intercourse into the lovemaking. The principles of focusing on sensation, mu-

tuality, communication, consideration, and relaxed pace must be carried over into sexual intercourse. It is best to begin with a position different from the one you have habitually used. Perhaps the most effective position and the one that allows the most pleasure for both partners is lying side by side. Each faces the other with legs intertwined; she lies on his thighs and one of his legs is between hers.

Again, this exercise will not eliminate all sexual problems. If you have conscientiously applied the techniques outlined here and are still unhappy with your sexual relationship, be sure to get outside help. The final chapter deals with where to go when all you've done isn't enough.

Once again, however, keep your expectations in line with reality! Be wary of assumptions that you must experience simultaneous, multiple orgasms while fireworks are exploding. Culturally created expectations may not be realistic, and the quality of the sex life must be determined by the partners involved.

CHAPTER 11

Some Final Thoughts

We got this far and thought our book was finished. We have covered the concepts and skills that are the most important for getting your marriage out of trouble. This is what we set out to do, and we have done it. However, in reading it over we realize we still have some thoughts and bases that haven't been covered. With apologies, therefore, for the important ones that are still left out, we'd like to offer up some final thoughts on secrets of a happy marriage. Though we openly admit that these are only our opinions and might not stand up to research, they are based on fourteen years in counseling and a combination of fifty-five years of marriage. Here, then, are Laura Ann and Cristy's final thoughts for keeping your marriage healthy:

1. Enjoy the simple pleasures again. As our world becomes more complicated it also becomes more sophisticated. We think it's time to get back to

simple pleasures—the ones that are free. A walk in the rain, lying before a blazing fire, watching the stars at night—these are the kinds of experiences that keep you in touch with yourself and your spouse.

2. Share the hard times, too. As important as it is to share the good times, we believe it's sharing the hard times that solidify your marriage. When the chips are down for your spouse, just be there. You don't need to offer advice, solutions, recriminations. Just be there!

3. Bring back the laughter and play. In the early days you and your spouse probably had lots of fun together: doing silly things, playing affectionate word games, and just horsing around. Bring back the crazy nicknames, outrageous ways of kidding, playful banter, childlike activities, laughter. It works wonders!

4. Learn to like yourself. It's when we don't feel good about ourselves that we don't feel good about our marriages. Low self-esteem leads to fear of rejection, possessiveness, jealousy, insecurity, and inability to take the risk of being known to your spouse. Recognize that you have worth simply because God made you. Tell yourself over and over, "I am unique. I am special. In all the world there is no one else exactly like me. I am OK." Love and affirm yourself. Get it from yourself, and it will come from others.

5. Get out of stereotyped roles. Ask yourself if old-fashioned ideas of masculinity and femininity are working for you. Does being a man mean being strong and silent, independent, domineering, emo-

tionless? Does being a woman mean being dependent, nonassertive, obedient, totally selfless, not responsible for your own life? If the answer is "yes," your "manhood" and "womanhood" are standing in the way of a better and closer marriage!

6. Stop listening to advice. All you have to do is say "I'm having trouble in my marriage" and everybody will stick their two-cents worth in—friends, relatives, co-workers, the butcher, the baker, the candlestick maker. It's mostly bad advice: "Dump the turkey, you're better off without him." "You'll love the swinging single life again." "You should see a lawyer and take him/her to the cleaners." "I wouldn't take that lying down." Tune the advice out. Listen to yourself. You are the only one who knows what is right for you.

7. Learn to forgive. The inability to forgive has broken up more marriages than you can ever know. Forgiving is marriage's toughest work. Many of you have been deeply, painfully, wounded by your spouse. You say you are willing to forgive and forget, but you just can't do it. It was unfair, the pain is too deep, you didn't deserve the hurt, and forgiveness comes hard. We suggest you begin to look at your spouse with different eyes. See him/her as a human, vulnerable, fallible, imperfect person like the rest of us. Every time you look through your new eyes and see your spouse as a weak, needy person who loves and needs you, instead of one who betrayed you, a little more weight will be lifted from your heavy heart. Remember the day in 1984 when Pope John Paul visited a prison in Rome. He took

161

the hand of Ali Agca, the man who had fired a bullet at his heart, and forgave him!

8. Speak of your spouse to others with love. Public affirmation of your spouse's good qualities will make him/her feel special and proud. Brag to other people about your spouse even if he/she is not around. The compliments will be even better when they get back to your spouse.

9. Carefully plan TV time. It would be fascinating to know how many marriages got into trouble because of TV! The world is full of people who use television to turn off their minds and shut out the world. It's their daily tranquilizer! The harmful side effect is often a broken marriage, however. You're shutting out your spouse along with the rest of the world. Do you walk in your den and automatically turn on the TV? What message does that give your spouse? A TV set in the bedroom is a painless way to avoid talking, making love, or facing your spouse if something unpleasant might come up. There's nothing wrong with TV if you plan ahead what you'd like to watch. Otherwise you can use it to avoid something that needs attention—your marriage!

10. Learn to "reframe" your complaints. Put a picture in a new frame and it can look like a new picture. Put your complaints in a new frame and you may not recognize them anymore. Bus drivers are taught to think that annoying passengers could perhaps be sick. You can likewise "reframe" your problems with your spouse. Qualities you like least in your spouse are often similar to those you like the best. You hate her stubbornness, but like her tenacity. Reframe her stubbornness as tenacity. He's ex-

plosive but delightfully spontaneous. Reframe his explosiveness as spontaneity. This goes beyond acceptance to learning to enjoy and affirm differences.

and finally . . .

11. Hang in there. Just say "I will stay," maybe for the hundredth time. In every long-term successful marriage there is at least one partner who is saying "I'm staying, no matter what comes. I married for better or worse, through thick and thin. This is for life." If you must leave, make sure, we mean 100 percent sure, that it will never work out. Don't make divorce just an unpleasant alternative: make it a last resort. We are called the dinosaurs now—the ones who married for life. It's a good feeling!

CHAPTER 12

When More Help Is Needed

We are not so naive as to believe that this book has solved all of the marital problems for everyone who has read it! We hope that it has solved all of the problems for some of you, and some of the problems for all of you. There are, however, some situations for which this book may not be enough. Now that you have started on the journey toward a happier marriage, continue it by getting more help if you need it.

Don't feel discouraged if you have tried everything in this book in good faith and still have major unresolved problems. There may be a number of reasons for this. The most basic is that we all have ego-defense mechanisms. These defense mechanisms work to protect our egos from painful, negative truths about ourselves. The truth literally hurts, so we rationalize, repress, project motivations on others, and do numerous other things that prevent us from seeing ourselves as we really are. These tendencies are human and are often below the level of consciousness. It is especially difficult to hear these truths from our spouses. If you believe that defense mechanisms are getting in the way of growth and change for either you or your spouse, you may need a trained, impartial counselor to help you over this hurdle.

There are any number of problems that for one reason or another are too difficult for a couple to solve on their own. Someone severely neurotic or someone who has experienced deep-seated problems for a number of years is not likely to be able to work through these problems alone. Clearly physical violence, child abuse, and alcohol and drug abuse are problems that require professional help. Also, persons experiencing severe depression, fear, or rage probably need help in working through these painful emotions. People dealing with trauma, such as rape, assault, sexual abuse, or incest are likely to need outside help, as will those suffering from unresolved grief from the death of a loved one. As we mentioned earlier, many problems with a couple's sexual relationship call for a trained therapist.

With this in mind we will direct you to finding someone who can help you if further help is needed. We'll speak first of the categories of helpers, and then where to find them. The following groups are all possibilities, but keep in mind that training and ability will vary tremendously within each category.

1. Psychiatrists: Psychiatrists are medical doctors and can prescribe medication (such as anti-depressants) when needed. Though their specialty is treat-

ing emotional problems, most have had little training in relationship counseling and actually prefer not to do it. There are psychiatrists who have a subspecialty in marriage and family counseling, however, and they are usually excellent choices. Warning: This is usually the most expensive route.

2. Counselors: This a broad territory and covers a bewildering array of background, training, and ability. Look for a doctorate in either counseling psychology or counselor education. Many states have either recently passed a counselor licensure law or have one in the making. Look for a license if your state is one of these. If not, the initials AAMFT (American Association for Marriage and Family Therapy) after a counselor's name is assurance he/she has met rigid requirements. Warning: Don't rule out those without the initials. Many excellent marriage counselors choose not to go through the expense of paying for the extensive and expensive required supervision beyond the college degree that AAMFT requires.

3. Clinical Psychologists: Clinical psychologists are trained in abnormal psychology and may be a good choice when there are very deep-seated problems. Again however, their interest in and training in relationship counseling should not be assumed.

4. MSWs: The Master of Social Work is the terminal degree in social work. It is a degree with an emphasis on therapy, and those holding it are often in private practice.

5. Minister/Pastoral counselors: Ministers usually know the family involved, and that can be an advan-

tage or disadvantage. If you are a member of the congregation, the counseling is usually free.

In every category above, the expertise, ability, training and interest in marriage counseling varies widely. Remember to ask what training a counselor has had in this area. Now that you have an idea of the kinds of marriage counselors available, the next step is to find one. We suggest the following:

1. Referrals: Your best bet is to find someone who can personally refer a marriage counselor to you. Obviously someone who has helped a friend or relative is the best recommendation. If you know no one who can refer a counselor, ask your doctor, lawyer, or minister for a recommendation. Finally, public school counselors often have contact with private practitioners and can be a referral source.

2. Local mental health centers: This can be a good starting point for inquiries if you can't find a personal referral. There are, however, advantages and disadvantages to going to a mental health center, so ask a lot of questions.

3. Yellow Pages: For obvious reasons, this can be risky. Nevertheless, most marriage counselors, competent and incompetent, are listed in the Yellow Pages under "Marriage and Family Counselors." The trick is to call as many as possible and ask many questions before you decide.

4. Professional organizations and directories: A number of professional organizations can direct you to their members in your area. AAMFT is your assurance of a well-trained marriage counselor. Some addresses are:

The American Association for Marriage and Family Therapy
1717 K Street N.W., Suite 407
Washington, D.C. 20006
Phone (202) 429-1825

American Mental Health Counselors Association
5999 Stevenson Avenue
Alexandria, Virginia 22304
Phone 1-800-354-2008

American Psychological Association
1200 Seventeenth St., N.W.
Washington, D.C. 20036
Phone (202) 955-7600

The American Association of Sex Educators, Counselors and Therapists
11 Dupont Circle, N.W., Suite 220
Washington, D.C. 20036
Phone (202) 462-1171

National Association of Social Workers
7981 Eastern Ave.
Silver Spring, MD 20910
Phone (301) 565-0333

5. Colleges and universities: There are many colleges and universities that train marriage counselors and offer marriage counseling by their trainees under supervision. This is usually at little or no cost, yet is excellently and carefully supervised.

Whatever you do, don't let one bad experience

with a counselor discourage you. If you end up with someone you can't relate to, who doesn't seem to understand you, or with whom you just aren't comfortable for whatever reason, have the courage to say good-bye and try another. There are enough terrific marriage counselors out there to make it crazy to stay with one who isn't helping you.

Good luck and lots of love. Our thoughts and prayers are with you!

Appendix
Worksheets and Forms

WIFE'S GOALS WORKSHEET

Category	Is this a problem?	Rank order of importance	What specific changes would you like?
Money			
Communications			
In-Laws			
Sex			
Religion			
Recreation			
Friends			
Alcohol and Drugs			
Children			
Jealousy			
Household Responsibilities			
Job			
Independence			

HUSBAND'S GOALS WORKSHEET

Category	Is this a problem?	Rank order of importance	What specific changes would you like?
Money			
Communications			
In-Laws			
Sex			
Religion			
Recreation			
Friends			
Alcohol and Drugs			
Children			
Jealousy			
Household Responsibilities			
Job			
Independence			

CATCH YOUR PARTNER PLEASING YOU

Name_____ Name of Partner_____

Day	Date	Pleasing behavior
Mon.		
Tues.		
Wed.		
Thurs.		
Fri.		
Sat.		
Sun.		
Mon.		
Tues.		
Wed.		
Thurs.		
Fri.		
Sat.		
Sun.		

HUSBAND'S SCRIPT WORKSHEET

What might your parents have said about . . .

	Mother	Father
Money		
Communications		
Sex		
In-Laws		
Religion		
Recreation		
Friends		
Alcohol and Drugs		
Children		
Household Responsibilities		
Work		
Personal Freedom		
Education		

What did you learn about marriage from your parents?

How did your father treat your mother?

How did you mother treat your father?

What was your father's role in the marriage?

What was your mother's role in the marriage?

How did your father handle conflict?

How did your mother handle conflict?

Did your father express angry, hurt, sad, or fearful emotions?

Did your mother express angry, hurt, sad, or fearful emotions?

Did your parents diplay affection for each other?

Did they display affection for you?

Were you able to express angry, hurt, sad, or fearful emotions as a child?

Who was the boss in your parents' marriage?

List any other script messages you may have gotten about these topics from other family members, friends, teachers, church, your race or ethnic background, or society's definition of masculine or feminine roles.

WIFE'S SCRIPT WORKSHEET

What might your parents have said about . . .

	Mother	Father
Money		
Communications		
Sex		
In-Laws		
Religion		
Recreation		
Friends		
Alcohol and Drugs		
Children		
Household Responsibilities		
Work		
Personal Freedom		
Education		

What did you learn about marriage from your parents?

How did your father treat your mother?

How did you mother treat your father?

What was your father's role in the marriage?

What was your mother's role in the marriage?

How did your father handle conflict?

How did your mother handle conflict?

Did your father express angry, hurt, sad, or fearful emotions?

Did your mother express angry, hurt, sad, or fearful emotions?

Did your parents diplay affection for each other?

Did they display affection for you?

Were you able to express angry, hurt, sad, or fearful emotions as a child?

Who was the boss in your parents' marriage?

List any other script messages you may have gotten about these topics from other family members, friends, teachers, church, your race or ethnic background, or society's definition of masculine or feminine roles.

TIT-FOR-TAT CONTRACT

Husband

The behavior that I have chosen to do for my wife is:

Signed:

Date:

_____

Wife

The behavior that I have chosen to do for my husband is:

Signed:

Date:

REWARD CONTRACT

Husband

The behavior that I have chosen to do for my wife is:

The reward I will receive for carrying out this contract is:

Signed:

Date:

Wife

The behavior that I have chosen to do for my husband is:

The reward I will receive for carrying out this contract is:

Signed:

Date: